TEACH Y...

C000027580

FUND RAISING

Tony Elischer

BA FICFM

all royalties go to

Imperial Cancer
Research Fund

Hodder & Stoughton

A MEMBER OF THE HODDER HEADLINE GROUP

This book is dedicated to
Nicky and Dorothy
without whom this project would not have been possible.

All author's royalties and fees from this book are being donated to the Imperial Cancer Research Fund, PO Box 123, London, WC2A 3PX. Tel. no. 0171 242 0200. Registered Charity Number 209631.

British Library Cataloguing in Publication Data

A catalogue record for this title is available from the British Library
ISBN 0 340 621133

First published 1995
Impression number   10 9 8 7 6 5 4 3 2 1
Year   1999 1998 1997 1996 1995

Typeset by Transet Limited, Coventry, England.
Printed in Great Britain for Hodder & Stoughton Educational, a division of Hodder Headline plc, 338 Euston Road, London NW1 3BH
by Cox & Wyman Ltd, Reading, Berks.

During the 30 years in which I was President of the Imperial Cancer Research Fund, I saw it grow from a relatively small charity spending less than £500,000 a year to become the fifth largest charity in the UK spending over £50 million each year. As a former President I have been able to see at first hand the immense impact a charity can have on peoples' lives.

None of the major advances made by the Imperial Cancer Research Fund in the prevention, treatment and cure of cancer would have been possible if it were not for the funds raised for the Charity from all sections of the population, using the full range of established and pioneering fund-raising techniques. Fund raising does not just happen. It requires the application of the skills, innovation and experience of dedicated individuals to make it work successfully.

In this book, Tony Elischer has used his and the Charity's knowledge of fund raising to provide a clear and accessible reference source for anyone contemplating starting or developing fund raising for their cause. I am delighted to commend this book to you. I am sure that it will help towards your fund-raising goals and ultimately benefit those in need.

Angus Ogilvy.

The Hon Sir Angus Ogilvy KCVO

About the author

Tony Elischer started his career in the dance and performing arts world. He gained practical experience in arts sponsorship and administration before moving to the charity sector. He has a track record in a comprehensive range of fund-raising techniques and has developed skills in many diverse areas.

Having identified the potential for corporate partnership opportunities for charities within the established and accepted fund-raising mix, he developed this area for the charity Help the Aged. After eight years there, he moved to the Zoological Society of London as Development Director. Here he developed an integrated fund-raising strategy to secure funds and support for the activities and capital projects of London Zoo and Whipsnade Wild Animal Park. He also devised and co-ordinated the Save Our Zoo campaign for London Zoo.

Tony Elischer then became Head of Fund Raising with the Imperial Cancer Research Fund. Having reviewed their fund raising to date, he created a new strategy for the division which involved a complete restructuring, resulting in a considerable growth in income from fund-raising activities year on year. He is now a senior consultant with The Management Centre, working with not-for-profit organisations worldwide.

The author has addressed a broad spectrum of international conferences, also written many papers and devised and run innovative workshops and training courses on many aspects of marketing and fund raising.

He is a trustee of the Fauna and Flora Preservation Society and advises many other charities in all aspects of fund raising.

CONTENTS

Acknowledgements

I would like to offer my special thanks to the following people for their generous contribution towards the writing of this book. Their expertise and guidance have been invaluable to me in developing and completing the project.

Nicola Elischer
Dorothy Harvey, Imperial Cancer Research Fund
Stephen Lee, Institute of Charity Fundraising Managers
Keith Mitchell, Imperial Cancer Research Fund
Jeremy Shaw, Smith, Bundy & Partners Ltd
Tom Smith, Smee and Ford Ltd

Thanks also to the following people for their help, support and input either in directly developing this book or in helping me to advance my knowledge, experience and enjoyment of fund raising over the years.

Ken Burnett (Burnett Associates), Alistair Collett (Wilde Sapte), Charity Commission, Joanne Horton-Hill (ICRF), John Mayo OBE (Help the Aged), George Medley, Redmond Mullin (Redmond Mullin Ltd), the National Fundraising Development Team (ICRF), Anna Nicholas (Anna Nicholas Associates), Freddie Phillips (ICRF), George Smith (Burnett Associates), Janet South (Help the Aged), Guy Stringer, Harold Sumption.

I would also like to mention with gratitude all the people I have worked with in fund raising over the years, and all my staff and colleagues.

INTRODUCTION

'People give to people first, whatever else second'

This book details all the basics you require to devise and implement a plan or activity to raise funds for your chosen cause. The key to the whole process, however, is *you*. Raising funds is a people business, full of some of the most persistent, enthusiastic, genuine and imaginative people you will ever meet. There are millions of different causes requiring support; but support is not automatic. People are necessary to promote the merits of each cause.

Since you are reading this book, you probably already have a cause that you wish to support, either as a volunteer or as a paid member of staff. These roles are vital to not-for-profit organisations in the United Kingdom. Having spent most of my professional life in fund raising, I know how difficult and challenging these roles can be. Most fund raising is an example of unique marketing expertise requiring individuals to master a series of skills. These skills range from writing a powerful direct mail appeal, to erecting a marquee or packing 5,000 envelopes on Sunday night for collection the following week. Even large charities will require you to become involved in a variety of jobs in order to gain the experience of the whole spectrum of charity techniques.

This book will provide you with an overview of the available methods for raising funds and enable you to select the appropriate technique for your own resources and skills. Very few of the techniques are mutually exclusive and you should view them as a series of building blocks towards achieving your goal. You need to be an opportunist to ensure that one gift leads to another and it is wise to regard your contact with donors as a long-term affair, building understanding, confidence and involvement. If you are new to fund raising, let your own knowledge develop gradually as you identify techniques that meet your immediate needs and start the fund-raising programme rolling. Concentrate on establishing these techniques as fully as possible, refining and developing them as you become more experienced.

Apart from the strict legal guidelines that govern fund raising in the United Kingdom, there are no other rules. The techniques in this book are drawn from years of experience in large national charities as well as local initiatives. The fund-raising environment changes constantly and requires a steady stream of new ideas to attract donors. Try to tailor techniques to your cause and add your own unique selling points (USP). It is vital to believe in your cause and then to adopt a positive attitude to raising funds. Negative states of mind regarding competition and the popularity or otherwise of your cause limit fund-raising ambitions; problems are not insurmountable if you are determined. Your role is to go as far as possible to meet the need and deal with the difficulties that will undoubtedly arise.

Putting the fun into fund raising is important when setting out to attract people to your cause and fund raising is more than just another job, whether paid or voluntary. Fund raising will offer you considerable enjoyment and fulfilment not always available in other jobs. For every 'Yes' there will be many a 'No', but you have the benefit of knowing that the results of all your efforts will help your chosen cause and effect a change.

Part One

GETTING STARTED

1

SETTING THE SCENE

Fund raising may be perceived as a relatively young profession, with many of the techniques still being developed and refined, however the origins of charity are firmly rooted in history. We can trace the awareness of the responsibility to help and support those in need back to ancient Greece and Rome, where charters were established to aid the poor and distressed. For centuries within the Jewish community there has been a tradition of charitable giving, raising funds through a carefully organised system which allows those who have to provide for those who those who have not.

Trusts and foundations, established to support needy causes, constitute a major element in charitable giving in the United Kingdom. Rules governing these bodies can be traced back to twelfth-century England and, in the reign of Elizabeth I, it was formally acknowledged that there was a need for favourable treatment for certain charitable purposes, under the Charitable Uses Act 1601.

There is no single definition of the word *charity* in English law, but in 1891 Lord MacNaghten classified charitable purposes as:

- relief of poverty
- advancement of education
- advancement of religion
- other purposes beneficial to the community.

In addition to this formal recognition, you will find the *Oxford English Dictionary* defining charity as: 'love of fellow men; kindness; leniency in judging others; liberality to those in distress, alms-giving, alms; institution or organisation for helping those in need, help so given'.

In the twentieth century, charities have mushroomed and charity law has continued to be refined and defined through the Charities Act 1960, the Charities Act 1992, Parts II and III, and the Charities Act 1993, which amalgamates the 1960 Act with Part I of the 1992 Act which is now the basis for charitable law in the UK. The contents of this book will reflect the legal requirements of the new Charities Act, but you will have to make more detailed reference directly to the legislation as your operation grows in scale and complexity.

At a conservative estimate there are currently around 275,000 registered charities and other voluntary organisations in England and Wales and, on average, there are 32 new ones registered every working day of the year. Of course, at the same time, some charity appeals cease and others relinquish their charitable status.

There are many, varying charitable causes which can be divided into the following diverse range of market segments:

- medicine and health
- general welfare
- international aid
- animal protection
- conservation and environment
- heritage
- religion
- youth and employment
- education
- the arts
- miscellaneous

The one thing that all causes have in common, whatever their segment of the market, is the need to fund their activities and therefore to raise funds.

—————— What is fund raising ——————

Fund raising is not an art limited to a chosen few and other brave souls who dare to play on the sidelines. Anyone who wishes to can become involved in fund raising as a volunteer, donor or organiser. People are the essential element in fund raising and, since most people enjoy dealing with other people, you should be able to find a role for yourself within this ever-growing and demanding field.

Fund raising is: the àrt of getting people to give you what you want; when and where you want it; for the purpose you have identified.

Getting people to give you what you want

Asking for something always seems to be the hardest thing for people to do; yet this is one of the most natural of human instincts; from the moment we are born, we make our wants and needs completely clear.

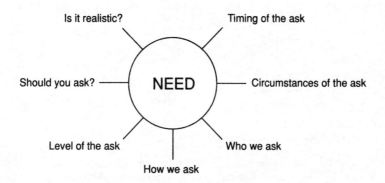

Figure 1 Factors that can affect the 'ask'

All of the factors in Figure 1 can affect your success in making the 'ask', yet most of these are assessed automatically, either in preparing to make the ask, or actually during the asking process:

- Who we ask: are they the right people for your cause or proposition?
- Circumstances of the ask: where is the best place to ask our potential donor, at home, work, or when involved in leisure activities?
- How we ask: face to face? by telephone? in a letter?
- Timing of the ask: is it a good time to approach potential donors?
- Is the ask realistic? Can the donor actually give or do what you are asking of them?
- Should you ask? Are you the best person to make the ask, or should you find a peer, a friend, or someone else the donor respects?
- Level: is the price of your ask right? Too high and you will fail, too low and you will sell yourself and your cause too cheaply.

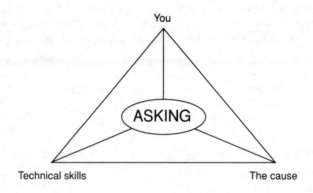

Figure 2 The three key elements that make up the ask

Making the ask is a mixture of three key elements. You should already possess two of these elements and, by the time you have read this book, I hope you will have absorbed the basis for the third, the necessary technical skills.

When and where you ask

This is affected by two things. First, how much time you have to raise the funds for a cause or project. Realistically, sound and successful fund raising is always planned with sufficient lead in time, and time for plans to take effect and produce the required funds. However, a sense of urgency will always aid an appeal. Secondly, by the technique you deploy, for any selected group of donors.

For the purpose you have identified

The cause motivates your need to raise funds and, therefore, must lead your fund raising at all times. On the basis that you feel strongly about a cause, it is likely that many others will feel the same, or can be motivated to do so. Therefore, as a fund raiser, you are an enabler, a catalyst affording people (donors), the opportunities to realise their ambitions, goals, life needs and purposes. When people hear the words *fund raising* they think of money, but fund raising is not only about money, it is about a cause needing support.

———————— The approach ————————

The most successful approach to fund raising is to reach as many people as possible, as often as possible, whatever their circumstances, with a proposition that makes them want to give. We will look at networks of people in more detail later, but consider the fact that any individual you interest in supporting your cause is the key to at least another 12 people.

- people they know
- people they knew
- people they know of.

How many commercial companies do you know who offer attractive incentives to introduce new customers? Like them, when it comes to reaching as many people as possible, you do not necessarily have to think big in terms of advertising and awareness, but you do have to think strategically about how you will encourage donors to help you reach more people. It may help at this stage to consider your donor more as a friend, because a donor will need to feel well cared for before they will introduce you to their own friends and contacts. Word of mouth is one of the most powerful marketing tools available to anyone in the charity or commercial world.

Reaching as many people as possible is important, but so is reaching existing donors as often as possible. A lot of new charities concentrate on continually recruiting new donors and supporters, but it is just as productive to work harder with the donors you have, to increase their value. Once you have acquired a reasonable and manageable number of donors, you should spend time learning about them and trying to understand why they support your cause. Then you may persuade them to give more often. Someone who has already given can be your most valuable asset, since they will be the person most likely to give again. Always remember you should only seek to recruit the number of donors that you can effectively service; do not overreach yourself or you may alienate potential support.

In figure 3 you can see the donor pyramid model that has been used successfully in fund raising throughout the world and illustrates how you should view your donors.

Figure 3 The donor pyramid

The general public constitutes a vast pool of opportunity. The charity aims to convert them into either:

Responders: those who respond to your various fund-raising techniques,

or

Enquirers: people who become aware of your work and activities who will contact you pro-actively.

In this way you will attract people who become donors and then give on a regular basis. Towards the top of the pyramid, a smaller group of people should move through to become committed givers and possibly major donors. You need to understand each of these donor tiers and build relationships with them, but the pyramid model reinforces the need to work on existing donors in order to reach the top of the pyramid, the ultimate fund-raising goal. You should also imagine a pyramid within each of these layers, as 80 per cent of your support will inevitably come from 20 per cent of your donors (the Pareto principle). The key to success is to identify and keep the 20 per cent.

Whatever their circumstances, as a fund raiser you are an intermediary, promoting the cause and enabling people to support it. You should create propositions and techniques that will reach the widest possible audience. Money may be the ultimate aim, but remember that successful fund raising is built on three key elements: time, money and goods. If you are a volunteer fund raiser, you have already committed the gift of time. Time and goods can lead ultimately to money, but they ensure that people who are motivated to help your cause can choose to do this in the way most appropriate to them, and people are not excluded merely because they cannot afford to donate money. All interest and help should be welcomed.

In fund raising there are four types of funding available:

- from gifts
- from grants
- from activities
- from investments.

On the assumption that most readers of this book will be taking their first steps in fund raising, only the first three sources of funding will be examined, since investments do not usually fall within the fund raiser's brief. Investment is a very specialised area needing a book in itself, although you should be aware of investments when looking at sources of funds for your charity.

The need to fund raise

This book is about learning to raise funds, but before you decide to do this, you must be clear about the 'need' for it. All successful fund raisers will tell you that their activities are needs led. It should be the need that motivates the fund raiser and this will in turn motivate the donor. You may be raising funds for an established charity, but it is up to you to ensure that you fully understand the need, in order to communicate it to others and create a relevant fund-raising programme. On the other hand, you may have been motivated to raise funds after identifying a particular need in society, but you will still need to spend time defining this and you should ask yourself:

- What is the need and why does it warrant support?
- How much money is needed and how will it be spent?
- What are the existing avenues of support for the need and how successful are they?
- Is the need being met elsewhere?
- Are there other existing bodies (charities, quangos, trusts, etc), who could help the need if asked and motivated ?
- Is there a time frame on the need? Is it realistic?
- What sort of funding is needed; is it capital or revenue?
- If it is a capital project, how accurate are the costings? Are they likely to go up?

These questions should give you an idea of how close an understanding of the need is required before you even begin to think about raising money. Competition in the voluntary sector is growing at an alarming rate, and a lot of time and energy must be invested in order to compete successfully. Therefore, the need must be explored in detail and clearly defined. Remember, *no need, no need to fund raise.*

Having defined the need, you will have reassured yourself that the money given by donors is essential to the cause and that it will be wisely spent. Once you have drawn public attention to the need, you then become the intermediary or facilitator who enables the donor to help. If there were no fund raisers, donors would still identify needs in society and choose to give, but fund raisers are agents of change in marketing these needs. The donor always has a choice of who to support and how, but charity fund raisers broaden the horizon and increase the knowledge of the various needs. Put yourself in the donor's place and ask – what makes you give?

2

STARTING A CHARITY

There are many not-for-profit organisations supporting every imaginable cause so, before you decide to set up a new one, investigate the possibilities of associating with an existing charity or other body that has similar objectives to your own. If this does not prove to be practical, and if it is appropriate, you may consider setting up as a registered charity. The checklist at the end of this section, and other relevant extracts, are taken from the Charity Commission's booklet *CC21 – Starting a Charity*, which will provide useful guidance for anyone considering setting up a charity.

Every voluntary organisation is not a charity. Any organisation that is wholly or in part commercial, political or for the benefit of private individuals is not eligible to register for charitable status, although it can become involved in raising funds.

There are four main categories that classify an organisation as a charity:

- the relief of the poor, handicapped or aged
- the advancement of education
- the advancement of religion
- other purposes beneficial to the community

There are many benefits of charitable status from a fund-raising point of view. These include:

- tax relief on income;
- ability to raise funds from other registered charities, e.g. trusts;

- some donors will have a policy of supporting only registered charities;
- the high regard the public have for a registered charity.

Registration

A new charity would normally be registered with the Charity Commission under one or more of the categories listed above, but there are exceptions to registration with the Commission; certain charities are classified as exempt or excepted, but in all cases it is wise to contact the Commission at an early stage to ensure that the correct registration procedure is followed.

If an institution is a charity and it is within the jurisdiction of the High Court then, with certain exceptions mentioned below, it must be registered with the Commission. Indeed, the trustees are under a legal duty to apply to the Commission for it to be registered.

Charities that are covered by the exceptions, and that do not have to register with the Commission, include:

- some voluntary schools;
- some small funds of the Scout and Guide Associations;
- certain charities for promoting the efficiency of the armed forces;
- some charities for the advancement of religion (see the Commission's leaflet *CC22*);
- places of worship registered under section 9 of the Places of Worship Registration Act 1855;
- charities which have none of the following:
  (a) permanent endowment (meaning property which cannot be spent as income); and
  (b) income above £1,000; and
  (c) the use or occupation of any land, including buildings.

An organisation set up to carry out work overseas can be charitable under English law. Its purposes must be ones which would be regarded as charitable if the organisation worked only in the United Kingdom. But an organisation set up to work in a particular foreign country will not be charitable if its purposes are illegal in that foreign country.

A legal structure needs to be established for the charity, and that structure should be the most appropriate one for the activities likely to be undertaken by the charity. The main types of legal structures for charities are:

- a charitable trust
- an unincorporated charitable association
- a charitable company.

Whatever the structure you decide upon, before you can register your new charity, a written governing document must be prepared. Model governing documents for all the above structures are available from the Charity Commission. Although you can adopt your own format for your charity's governing document, the registration process is likely to progress more quickly and smoothly if the document is produced in a form already agreed as acceptable by the Commission.

Every charity must have trustees. Charity trustees are described in the 1993 Charities Act as 'the persons having the general control and management of the administration of a charity'. The role and duties of trustees are covered in the section below. See also Charity Commission leaflet *CC3 – Responsibilities of Charity Trustees*.

The actual registration process follows the pattern outlined below:

- completion of initial questionnaires from the Charity Commission;
- submission of draft document;
- the Commission invites the charity's registration;
- a completed registration application form and a copy of the charity's governing document are sent to the Commission;
- the charity is entered onto the Register and the registered number is issued.

After registration, the trustees are responsible for providing annual accounts and an annual return, which justifies the charity's work against its stated objects, to the Charity Commission (see leaflet *CC25 – Charity Accounts*); and for notifying them of any alterations to the charity's governing document or registered details.

Trustees

There are currently about one million people in England and Wales fulfilling the important role of charity trustee. The 1993 Charities Act has clearly defined the quite considerable legal liabilities of charity trustees and, therefore, the role should not be undertaken lightly. With a few exceptions, this is a position that anyone is legally eligible to take on. However, careful consideration should be given to what a person can actually contribute to the charity before they are invited to become a trustee. It is important that all trustees can give the required time to their role and that they have an interest in the charity's area of work. They should be able to contribute positively to the charity through their skills and experiences, but they may not make a financial profit from their role. They should have a comprehensive knowledge and understanding of the work of the charity, its charitable aims and objectives and of the charity's governing document.

The main duties are of a trustee are:

- to attend the meetings of the board of trustees
- to ensure that the actions of the charity and the trustees are in line with the governing document
- to administer the charity
- to manage the finances of the charity
- to make the appropriate returns to the Charity Commission and any other relevant bodies.

The annual accounts form the main return to be made by the charity and the level of income dictates the type of return that has to be made to the Charity Commission. For example, a charity (not a charitable company), having an income of under £100,000, is only required to submit a simple form of independently checked accounts. (The required format is available from the Commission.)

If the charity ceases to exist or to operate, the trustees must write to the Commission sending a copy of the charity's final accounts and a copy (confirmed as correct) of the minutes of the meeting at which it was resolved that the charity be dissolved or wound up. The charity can then be removed from the Register.

Checklist of questions for charity promoters

An extract from the Charity Commissioners' booklet Starting a Charity (CC21), available from The Charity Commission (See Appendix 2)

The role of existing charities

1 Is there an existing charity, voluntary organisation or statutory body in the area already doing the same or similar work? If so, is there a need for a new charity?
2 If a new charity is needed, have you discussed co-operation with any existing charity, organisation or statutory body to ensure that you do not simply duplicate their efforts?

Aims and objectives

3 What exactly is the purpose or object of the charity to be? This needs careful thought at the outset, so that the purposes of the new charity can be clearly and precisely set out. A lack of clarity in this area could lead to later problems and could thwart the original intentions.

Activities

4 What activities will be carried out to achieve that purpose or object? It may be sensible to mention specific activities among the powers which the trustees may exercise in carrying out their purposes.
5 Will the benefits of the charity be restricted to people living in a particular area or place? If so, this should be included within the purposes of the charity.

Finance and funding

6 How will you obtain the funds required to run the charity?
7 Will you need grants from central or local government or other charities and, if so, are they likely to be made available?
8 Will you have to raise funds directly from the public? (See leaflet *CC20, Fundraising Charities.*)

9 Are you satisfied that enough funds are available now, and will be in the future, to pay for planned activities?

Trustees should be careful not to commit themselves to any substantial expenditure unless they have the required funds or funds have actually been made available to them. If the charity does not have sufficient funds to honour a commitment, trustees may find themselves personally liable for work done on the charity's behalf or for goods supplied to it.

Land and buildings

10 Where will the charity operate from?

11 Will you need to rent, lease or buy premises?

12 Will suitable premises be available? If a charity will need to own or rent property, the governing document should included a power for the trustees to acquire property.

Governing document

13 What type of structure (a trust or an unincorporated association or a company) will be the most suitable for the charity? Have you received expert advice – perhaps from a national co-ordinating body or a lawyer? It is important that the correct structure be chosen at the start, because it will be difficult to change it later and the charity will need to be re-registered if its structure is changed.

14 Is there a model governing document for this type of charity? If there is, then the Commission recommends that it be used.

Trustees

15 How many charity trustees will be needed to manage the charity? There should be a minimum of three, but not so many that it becomes impossible to hold quorate meetings or to reach clear management decisions. Trustees should be at least 18 years of age.

16 Are you satisfied that the trustees have the skills needed to run a charity? if the charity is to provide specialised services, or to handle large amounts of property or investments, then trustees with relevant skills should be appointed.

17 Have any people been asked if they wish to become the first trustees and, if so, have they agreed to act? Are they aware of the responsibilities of charity trustees? New trustees should always be given:

(a) a copy of leaflet *CC3 Responsibilities of Charity Trustees*;

(b) a copy of the charity's governing document;

(c) copies of the minutes of any committee or group formed to set up the charity.

18 Has each of the proposed trustees been asked to confirm that he or she is not disqualified from acting as a charity trustee? It is an offence for a disqualified person to act as a trustee. This is intended to reduce the risk of someone becoming a trustee who may have a history of dishonesty, financial incompetence, or misuse of charity property.

Staff

19 How many (if any) professional and other staff will the charity have to employ? If the charity is to employ staff, a power to do this should be included in the governing document.

Membership

20 Will the charity have a membership and, if so, how will this operate? If the charity is to have members, then the governing document will have to say:

(a) how a person can become a member;

(b) what functions the members will have in the running of the charity;

(c) what relationship the members will have with those responsible for managing the charity (i.e trustees);

(d) how and when the membership will meet.

3

ESTABLISHING A FUND-RAISING OPERATION

There are many practicalities to be dealt with when setting up your fund-raising operation and careful consideration should be given to what is needed.

Resources

Where will you operate from?

You need an address and telephone number as the official contact point for the charity or organisation. This can be a private house or a local office. When deciding on this contact point, estimate the likely level of correspondence and telephone calls; can you acquire low cost or free appropriate office space? Decide whether you need the accommodation for a short or long term?

Whether you are organising a one-off event or are setting up a long-term operation, you will certainly need an operating base, even if it is only for receiving mail or for storing fund-raising leaflets.

If you are going to use a private address you will need to ensure that appropriate space and time are available. For example, if you are using the telephone number as a contact number is there someone there to take the calls or is an answerphone available? Should you decide you only need an address for correspondence, a local company may be prepared to act as your mailing point. However, if it is likely that you are going to be widely publicising the contact details and are setting up for a longer period, you may want to establish an office for your organisation, and there are several options for securing this at little or no cost. A local company may donate the office space, or the Local Authority may help out; you may be able to use surplus space at the neighbourhood charity shop or it might be possible to share the office with another group or organisation.

What equipment is needed?

This obviously depends on the level and type of operation but likely requirements will include:

- basic furniture
- a telephone with an answerphone
- appropriate storage space
- letterhead paper.

When having your letterhead printed, include all the relevant registration information and a fund-raising statement or message, so avoiding VAT on printing costs. You may also need to consider facsimile machines and photocopiers, but in the initial stages you could use a local bureau for these facilities. Depending on the scale of the operation, you may need a computer or word processor since you will certainly need to produce letters.

What human resources are needed?

The simple answer to this question is – the right level for the work to be done. The basic requirement will probably be someone to deal with telephone queries, and the appropriate level of cover can be provided by one or several volunteers. However, you will also need to consider what other skills or expertise you may need.

Given these main areas of consideration, list down what you need for your specific operation in terms of premises, equipment, people. Then list those you already have, or ideas for obtaining them, and match up the two lists.

Finance

When you have a clear idea of your resource requirement, you need to estimate the costs involved. This estimate should include on-going costs, not just the setting up and purchase costs.

If you are starting up a new organisation with a few other people, you may consider financing these set up costs yourselves as your contribution to the cause; or you may be able to identify statutory or other grants for which you could apply. If you are setting up a new group for an already established organisation, you may receive an initial amount from the central body. As your fund raising progresses, you may use some of the funds generated for essential running costs. However, to be able to do this you will have to have received at least some general donations, that is money that has been given to further the charity in general and not for a specific purpose or project.

Wherever you get financing from, you need to be aware that you are using money that has been given to a cause and you are accountable for its effective use. All monies should be properly and clearly accounted for and accounts should be produced that are available for scrutiny. This is an area in which donors are rightly interested, and every effort should be made to keep cost ratios down, to ensure that the maximum level of funds are available for the cause for which they were given. Every charity has to produce annual accounts for the Charity Commission. Organisations registered elsewhere also have to make relevant returns.

—— Basic administration systems ——

To ensure that your fund raising operates effectively, appropriate administration systems will have to be established and adhered to.

Keeping Records

There are various ways of keeping efficient records and some of the things that should be recorded are:

1   Telephone calls: the time and date of the call; the name and number of the caller and their organisation or company if appropriate;

the subject of the call and the action taken.

2 Event records: these should include all the details of the event with contact names, addresses and telephone numbers; lists of the participants and sponsors; all approaches for support and the outcome; an event report with the results of the event and recommendations.

3 Donor records: full details of any individual, group, company, trust or organisation that has donated; include details of the donation and any special information. Also keep notes of approaches that have been rejected.

4 Income and expenditure records: details of incomings and outgoings of the organisation.

5 Project and campaign records: these should contain comprehensive details of any project and project summaries; they will provide useful information for similar future projects.

Keeping accurate, up-to-date records is crucial to the successful running of an organisation. They ensure that every donation has been appropriately acknowledged; that all leads have been effectively followed up and that useful information is available to all the people working for a cause. All records should be kept in a logical way to allow for easy access.

Reactive fund raising

When people write or telephone, consider each request or opportunity in the light of its fund-raising potential. Sometimes a simple fund-raising idea can be extended into a regional or national campaign.

Quality of service is something we look for as consumers every time we spend money; make sure your office and fund raisers always offer the highest possible level of service to donors and supporters.

4
STRATEGIC PLANNING

When you know what you want to do, you must define how you are going to do it. In other words you need a strategic plan; simply put, this is a road map to help to reach the final goal. Some parts of the plan will work well, others may not, but by having a guiding outline it is possible to change direction, adapt and up-date the route, yet still reach the final destination.

Mission and vision

Review your research into the *need* and identify your *mission* and your *vision*. The mission should reflect the aims of your organisation in one or two sentences (the shorter the better), and the vision is where you want to be and what you want to achieve. Remember the *KISS* principle, *Keep It Short and Simple*. It takes time to create the right statements, but it is surprising how useful they can become and the variety of uses you will find for them. Try to make your statements as distinctive as possible, in order to stand out from the crowd and to help the public to remember your organisation and its aims. The mission and the vision are best developed by a small working party representing all aspects of your cause.

Environment

The second part of your plan should be a short review of the environment and general market place in which your organisation will be operating. This need not be lengthy, but it helps to identify any problems or advantages that you will face in the short to medium term. It also serves to remind others joining your cause of how you and your initial committee perceive the environment in which you are trying to achieve your vision. Some of the key areas on which you should comment are:

- Competitors: who are they and how well established are they? How active are they and are they a threat to your activities and sources of funds? Are they likely to co-operate with your future plans?
- Economy: what are the pressures on people's finances and what is employment like in your area? Are the local businesses thriving?
- Political: what government support is currently given to your generic cause, on a national or local basis? What is happening in local government and what is the attitude of government to your area of work?

You could also include some background on society's view of your cause and any other factors you consider to be relevant or important.

SWOT analysis

The next stage in support of your strategic plan is to draw up a SWOT analysis of your organisation, i.e. a diagram outlining its Strengths, Weaknesses, Opportunities and the Threats against it. This is a universally used technique for testing and developing a strategic plan. Identify the four sections:

- Strengths: what are the major selling points and what assets do you feel the organisation has in its favour? These can be drawn from positioning in the market, personnel, reputation, etc.
- Weaknesses: the opposite of the strengths outlined above; the areas that need strengthening, developing or initiating.

The second section of the diagram deals with external factors that affect your organisation, either positively (opportunities) or negatively (threats).

- Opportunities: from your general review of the market place, what do you see as the major opportunities and openings for the organisation?

- Threats: which outside factors will need to be monitored to ensure that they do not adversely affect the organisation or its fund raising?

Many people undertake SWOT analysis in a brainstorming situation and lay it out on a flip chart:

strengths	weaknesses
opportunities	threats

I have used the SWOT analysis for many years, although I feel it should really be called the TOWS analysis because it can be easier to complete the exercise by starting from the outside factors and working in. Your analysis should be reviewed regularly, and it is also a useful way of reviewing individual fund-raising techniques and opportunities.

Objectives

Defining the key objectives is the fourth part of the plan. All objectives must relate to the mission statement and lead to your vision. After each objective you should outline how you propose to achieve it (key tasks). If you are new to fund raising, the rest of this book should equip you with the knowledge to fulfil many of your objectives. You will need to gain a basic understanding of each available fund-raising technique before outlining your plans.

To monitor and measure the success of your activities, it is necessary to develop a means of measuring each objective. Each one should be assigned to a group or an individual, with a clear briefing of how their contribution fits into the overall plan. By allocating each task, you will see how far your existing resources will stretch and whether you need to recruit more volunteers, employ more staff or seek the input support of a consultant.

Timetable

All of this can be then set into a timetable of activities, preferably in a linear form, so that you can easily see what should be happening and how each objective impacts on another. Use a sheet of A3 paper to list key tasks in the left hand column. Mark the start times and completion dates of each task and use a dotted line to indicate preparation times.

Example

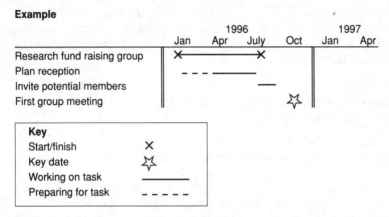

Figure 4 Linear calendar

This is an academic exercise in the early stages, but is does give you a broad picture to work to, and can be revised as you progress. As you gain experience, you will refine the process and it will soon become a useful working tool for your own fund raising and for the organisation as a whole.

Finances

The final section of your plan deals with finances and should complement the words with figures. How much are your plans going to cost? Include all the necessary elements in the calculation, e.g. salaries, office costs, direct fund-raising costs, publicity and consultancies. It is always better to be pessimistic rather than optimistic with costings and remember to build in a small contingency allowance.

Next try to assess the level of income. Place a conservative figure on the various fund-raising activities you propose. There may be people within your organisation who have experience of charities or other voluntary bodies, who could help you to draw up a general guideline to income. Never undertake any fund raising without forming an idea of how much you expect to raise, since this regulates your expenditure and use of resources. Large charities set targets for their fund raisers, on the basis of the type of activity and the stage of its development.

When you have completed your first draft of the budget, you can consider your cost ratio, which tells you how much it is going to cost you to raise raise each £1. Simply divide your expenditure by your income to discover this figure.

Example:

Expenditure £350 ÷ Income £2,000 = 17.5%
Therefore it costs 17.5 pence to raise each £1

You can apply this cost ratio analysis to all of your fund raising and to each individual activity. Remember that, in the first two years, your cost ratio may be higher than your ideal level, but this allows for initial start up costs. Different types of fund raising will always carry different cost/income levels. The key is to know this and to budget accordingly. Cost ratio is an important measurement and one that your donors will wish to know about, i.e. 'How much reaches the cause as opposed to being spent on administration?'

Figure 5 The cost ratio of fund-raising techniques

Once you have completed an overall budget for the first year, it is important to divide it up into monthly segments, both for income and expenditure. This helps to monitor the organisation on a monthly basis and it will help you you to foresee cash flow problems. While it is all very well to project a large income in the medium or long term, this can only happen if your short-term cash and resources are sufficient to finance your activities. The cash flow will also help you to determine the appropriate technique for raising funds speedily. You may need to devise techniques, such as collections, that will bring in short-term funds to finance the long-term activities.

The type of appeal you are running will decide how far ahead you can afford to plan, but most people work on a three to five year basis. Remember that some of the techniques you propose may take a year or more to develop.

There is very little difference between running a successful business and running a voluntary organisation; the business is driven by the need for profit and a charity needs to support its activities. (If you do your job properly in a charity, you should work yourself out of a job.) If companies could work to the same cost ratio as charities, they would have ecstatic share holders, since charities need to achieve a better cost ratio than a business in order to succeed, and this requires sound planning. All major charities have detailed strategic plans used as working tools in their day-to-day activities. There is no difference when it comes to small or medium sized charities, since they may be the large charities of tomorrow.

Part Two

THE TECHNIQUES

5

COLLECTIONS AND EDUCATION

There are many fund-raising techniques, from collections to capital campaigns; from trusts to trading. The Institute of Charity Fund Raising Managers (ICFM), calculate that there are approximately 23 generic techniques or constituencies from which hypothetically you can raise funds. A successful fund-raising programme will rely on the correct and appropriate use of a mix of techniques. It is important to understand each method of fund raising to ensure that the right technique is used in the most effective way. Your strategic planning exercise will have enabled you to decide upon the most appropriate techniques and the order in which to use them. There is a natural temptation to choose the way of fund raising with which you are most familiar, but no technique should be dismissed until you have thoroughly explored what it offers. In the following pages I will look at each technique in detail to allow you to make informed decisions on which is best for you and for your cause.

We have established that there is a huge choice available when it comes to deciding how you are going to raise money but on the other hand all the techniques rely on one, or a combination, of three factors – time, money and goods.

Time

People can give their time to help raise funds for your cause or to save on expenditure. They can, among other things:

- act as a steward at an event
- stand on a street corner with a collecting tin
- sell tickets for an event or raffle
- serve on a stall or in a charity shop
- be a member of an organising committee, or start a committee
- offer help in a professional capacity
- participate in a sponsored event.

Money

This is the one that people think of first when you mention fund raising, and again there are many ways that people can give money to a cause (and the more ways they are offered the better). People can, among many other things:

- put money in an envelope or collecting can
- buy an item from a stall, shop or catalogue
- leave a legacy
- make a covenant
- sponsor someone to participate in an event
- provide sponsorship for an event
- participate in a payroll giving scheme.

Goods (gifts in kind)

There are many situations in which the donation of goods to a cause can be a valuable part of your fund raising. Either to be used directly by your cause or to instigate or enhance further fund raising. You should provide as many opportunities as possible for people to give in this way. They can, among other things:

- provide items to be sold in a shop or on a stall, either by donating or making items
- give prizes for a raffle, tombola, etc.
- donate the use of facilities for an event, e.g. swimming pool, sports stadium
- provide office space, equipment or services, e.g. printing
- provide equipment for use at an event, e.g. public address system, bouncy castle

- companies can donate suitable excess stock for sale or use
- provide items to be used by the cause, e.g. furniture for a day care centre, toys for a playgroup.

All of the techniques I am going to analyse have time, people and resource implications and need to be considered in line with your fund-raising strategy and your circumstances. However, you will see that every appeal has access to a wide portfolio of techniques that will meet the needs and ensure that fund raising is challenging, enjoyable and exciting.

Collections

The vast majority of people will have some experience and understanding of collections, as they are widely employed by charities of all sizes. In many cases this knowledge will come from first-hand experience – that is to say that will have either given to a charity via a collection or very possibly have acted as a collector at some time. Collections originally consisted of church giving in the form of the collection plate, tithes, alms, etc. Today the idea remains the same, but the large number of charities involved in this method of fund raising demands a sophisticated approach and meticulously planned organisation in order to guarantee success.

Although collections vary in format, with varying advantages and disadvantages, there are certain features common to all:

- they use a receptacle for the collection
- they provide a wide opportunity for donors to give and comment
- they generally expect small amounts, but never exclude the possibility of larger donations
- they provide an opportunity for making the cause more widely known
- most need collectors.

House to house

(The ICFM publish a Code of Practice for house-to-house collections).

A collector goes to every house in a given area either asking for a donation or, as in most cases, delivering and later collecting a collection device, usually a small envelope. Before this stage is reached, however, there is much to be done and all activities should be planned well in advance.

First, decide the area in which you want to run your house to house collection. If you are fund raising for a very local cause the area of the collection will probably be the immediate vicinity of your town or village. It is necessary to consider what effect the project may have on a wider area and, if it will serve a wider community, you may wish to run collections in surrounding towns as well. National charities tend to operate across the whole of the country and many use a rolling programme, collecting in different areas at different times of the year; or they plan their collection around block periods, e.g. Christian Aid in May, British Legion in November. Unless the charity for which you are organising the collection holds a Home Office Exemption Order (this will transfer to the Charity Commission once Part III of the Charities Act 1992 is in force), it is illegal to collect without the permission of the local District Authority's licensing department who control all collections held in public places. Permission for collections in London is given by the Metropolitan Police.

Book the dates for your collection with the District Council and, wherever possible, avoid the weeks when other charities have already booked their collections. Once you have the required authority to collect, acquire a good up-to-date street map. You should divide up the area into sections to be covered by each collector, ensuring that no one person has too much to do and that you have selected the areas from which you would expect the highest return. This will require some thought and a degree of local knowledge. Give consideration to the type of housing in each section, e.g. houses that have individual drives will take longer for a collector to get round than those that are closer to the road, and be aware of sheltered housing and old people's homes, etc.

You then need to recruit your collectors, who should be reliable and must be over 16 years of age. There are many ways of doing this and the best way will depend on the individual situation. If you have a local group or committee it may be possible for you to divide up the area between the group members, other regular volunteers, their friends etc. You could enlist the help of a local organisation or you may wish to advertise for helpers in the library, local shops and even the local newspaper. Many of the larger charities use electoral registers and the telephone book to secure local collectors over the telephone. Good practice guidelines for recruitment of collectors by telephone are produced by the ICFM.

When you have your collectors organised you have to ensure that they have the appropriate materials to carry out the collection. They will need:

- the right number of envelopes for the area they are covering with enough 'spares' for the people who will have inevitably misplaced their original envelope. Non exemption holders need special permission for use of envelopes;
- a collector's authorisation card/badge showing that they are a bona fide collector for the charity. The card will also carry details of the area to be covered and the dates during which the collection can take place.
- information on the charity and details of the collection.

Your volunteer collectors need a contact name, address and telephone number should any queries arise. They will need confirmation of the area they are covering and instruction on what to do with the money collected. This could be to take the sealed envelopes to a central collecting point (a local bank or building society may be prepared to help you); or to deliver the envelopes to you or another member of your group. Anyone who is involved in opening the envelopes and counting the money has to do so in the presence of an independent witness. Collectors should also be provided with information about the cause for which they are collecting.

The materials used for your house to house collection provide many valuable opportunities for giving information about your cause and increasing awareness of it. The envelope itself should be eye-catching with a strong brief message clearly displayed; here is an opportunity to tell potential donors what their donation can buy, e.g. £1 can provide . . . Space can be provided for further information to be requested or so that people can volunteer to become involved with the charity or donate in a different way. Do remember that *all* materials should bear the address of the charity and *must* include the registered charity number, and a statement identifying the organisation as a registered charity. After the collection is completed a full return has to be made to the authority that granted permission to collect. This will detail the names and addresses of all collectors and the amount they collected from a particular area. All collectors should be thanked for their help. This can be done individually or as a group if this is more appropriate. A letter in the local paper, thanking everyone who gave and giving the total amount raised, is a good way of letting everyone involved know how the collection went, as well as providing additional profile for your cause.

Much of the information you will have gained will be useful to you for future collections or other activities. Details of volunteers who collected, donors who made enquiries, etc, should all be kept for later reference.

HOUSE TO HOUSE SUMMARY

- gain the appropriate permission
- carefully and accurately divide up the area
- recruit volunteer collectors
- acquire and distribute the required materials to the collectors
- make banking arrangements
- complete the returns
- thank everyone.

Street collections

There are many similarities between street collections and house to house collections. You will need to obtain permission from the District Council to hold a street collection and the date for it will have to be booked with them. This will have to be done well in advance as the popular days, e.g. Saturdays, market days, will be taken up quickly. If you are going to organise this type of collection you want to ensure the maximum return so do give careful consideration not only to the best day of the week but also the best time of year to hold your street collection.

You will need to recruit and organise a group of volunteer collectors and they must be over 16. These volunteers will have to stand in the street with a collecting device and donation acknowledgements for a period of time and, whilst they cannot actually ask for money, they should be prepared to attract the attention of passers-by by taking up a prominent position, smiling and generally making contact with people.

You will need enough collectors to give good coverage of the main areas of the town and each collector should do a two hour shift. Therefore, well before the collection day you should visit the town and decide where to station the collectors. Consider which shops attract the largest number of customers. Are there access points to car parks? Where are the popular places for lunch? Mark your chosen positions on your town map and code each position. Then draw up a rota ensuring each position is covered for the optimum amount of time.

When a volunteer agrees to collect make sure you reconfirm this to them in writing, giving details of where to report, where they will be collecting and the times that they will be on duty. You should ensure that they report in at least 15 minutes before the start of their shift. All collectors should be supplied with a collection authority and know exactly what is expected of them.

You will need to consider a suitable site for your command headquarters. Somewhere central where collection materials and money can be securely stored and where your volunteers can check in. It is also a good idea to be able to provide hot or cold drinks as appropriate for your helpers. Obviously this site will need to be manned at all times for reasons of security and in case of queries.

Then there are the materials to be used. The collecting device has to be practical, secure and attractive. There are many different types of collecting tin available and you will need to decide which best suits your needs. If you are likely to be using the cans on several occasions then you should chose a sturdy, reusable model. If, however, this is to be a one off you may decide to use a cheaper disposable alternative. Whatever the case the law requires that the device must be sealed; it is illegal to use an open tin or bucket. Make the most of the tin to advertise the cause – a short memorable line can be good motivation for people to give, e.g. Help Fight Cancer, or Help Save a Child's Life, etc. Remember, in a street collection a donor only has a split second to decide to support your cause before they have passed the collecting tin. Your collectors can wear brightly coloured sashes, baseball caps or something similar, bearing the name of the charity.

Are people going to be given an aknowledgement of their donation? Again there are many possibilities available, ranging from a simple sticker with the charity's name on, to a symbol of the cause, e.g. a poppy. Having these aknowledgements printed will be the main expense (as you can sometimes borrow collecting tins), and you should weigh up the cost of the stickers against the size of the collection or the level of activity you are likely to undertake in the collection area.

Awareness of what your street collection is for is very important. In addition to strong branding on the collection itself, you can also ask local newspapers to run a story in advance and for a local radio station to put out reminders on the day – you might even get an interview.

Accurate records of the street collection must be kept and a return made to the appropriate District Council. This should include details of all collectors and the amount they collected in their tin. (As with house to house collections, tins should be opened and monies counted in the presence of an independent witness.) Do ensure that you keep this information for yourself, as those names and addresses will be useful to you in the future. Everyone involved should be thanked for their participation in the collection.

STREET COLLECTION SUMMARY

- gain the appropriate permission
- plan the collection sites
- recruit the volunteers
- find a central control base
- get the required materials
- arrange banking
- complete the necessary records
- thank everyone.

Private property collections

These are the same as street collections, except that they are held on private property such as a privately owned shopping centre or a large supermarket. You do not need to apply for a permit for these collections, only the permission of the company operating the site is required, and you will normally get this after an initial letter or telephone call to the general manager of the site. Although many of the major supermarket chains now adopt a national charity for the year, local store managers will still usually allow some collections for local causes.

Again, you will need a group of volunteers who are prepared to collect for a given amount of time and using the same materials as for a street collection.

These private property collections often offer a good opportunity for promoting the cause via some sort of display. This could be a simple table (with a banner bearing the name of the charity and some information on the cause), to a larger display with photographs, posters and anything else that will catch the eye. Having some of your collectors in fancy dress can be a good attention grabber, even better if the costume in some way relates to the cause, e.g. animal costumes for an animal welfare charity.

As with all collections it is important that everyone is thanked for their part in the day, especially the person giving permission for the collection since you may well want to repeat the event. The store will also like to know how much was raised and a poster for the staff room will not go amiss. These collections can be a valuable source of funds and, therefore, it is extremely important to maintain good relations with the store staff throughout your collection and to ensure that your collectors do not interfere with the normal trading activity in any way, i.e. by obstructing doorways, trolley parks etc.

PRIVATE PROPERTY COLLECTIONS SUMMARY
- gain the appropriate permission
- recruit the collectors
- look at publicity/display opportunities
- decide on the siting of collectors and display
- get the required materials
- arrange banking
- thank everyone.

Static collecting boxes

(The ICFM produce guidelines on the use of static collecting boxes.)

These collections do not require a collector to hold the device. In fact here the device (and its positioning) is the key to success. It has to attract the attention and motivate the donation. There are an enormous variety of these static devices available from specialist manufacturers. However, if you only require a small number you could ask a local college or school to make one or two eye-catching, unique examples. Make sure you look at existing boxes when considering designs. Remember the law requires that all collecting devices bear the registered charity number.

Counter-top devices

These can be as simple as a collecting tin similar to the ones used for street collections placed on a shop counter – here you are simply relying on the cause or name of the charity to solicit the donation. To attract a greater number of donations, however, it is worth considering some sort of interactive device. We are familiar with the little lifeboat that launches when a coin is deposited in the RNLI box and the boxes that zig zag the coin through a circus or jungle scene. These are clearly designed with children in mind who will watch the activity and want to repeat the experience.

Stand-alone devices

These are in general larger collecting boxes, and will stand on the ground outside a shop entrance for example. They can be in the shape of an animal (WWF's panda) or a children's character (NSPCC's Postman Pat). There are also the more permanent stand-alone devices, like the wishing well in the public gardens, or the Second World War mine on the sea front.

Some of these static boxes offer a donation acknowledgement. This can be in the form of a sticker held in the base of the device. In the United States some now respond to a deposited coin with a Thank You or a flashing light.

Although these devices do not require a collector to hold them, they do need someone to service them. The money collected needs to be counted, receipted and banked on a regular basis. A full or overflowing collection box may suggest the charity is not in real need of funds. It is always worth asking whether somebody on the premises where your box is sited would be responsible for contacting you if the box needs emptying before your next scheduled visit. The positioning and condition of the device should be regularly checked. A tatty collecting box, or one that is hidden away in a dark corner with several others, is not giving the right messages about your cause. Therefore, a relationship needs to be developed with the person who has given permission for the siting of the box, and a regular contact should be established to ensure the best returns.

The positioning of the device is of considerable importance. If a box is sited by a till, people are going to have coins available in their hand. A static device placed where people are going to be queueing is likely to be more popular than one where people are merely passing by. A good position for your collecting box can make a considerable difference to the return you can expect, so do give this careful thought.

It is a sad fact that security is now a major consideration. Counter-top boxes should be secured to the counter where possible; stand-alone devices should also be chained or fixed down.

STATIC COLLECTIONS SUMMARY
- gain the appropriate permission
- consider and acquire the most appropriate collecting device
- position the device carefully
- arrange servicing for the device
- thank the box holder regularly.

Other collections

Collections at events

For this type of collection the first thing you need is research and local knowledge. You need to find out about any events that happen locally, consider the possibilities for a collection and find out who can give permission to collect (venue manager or event organiser if the event is to be held on private property. If, however, the event is to be held in a public place, you will also need a collecting permit).

A collection can be organised at almost any activity that people attend; some offer greater opportunities than others. For example, if you have local football teams, a premier league team is likely to give you a higher return than a third division team and a premier game against a big name team is likely to be better than one against a club that attracts few supporters; a local derby game would probably be a very good bet. Organisers of some events who give permission to collect may also allocate a number of free tickets for your collectors. These can be an important incentive and a valuable thank you.

Look at all the possibilities: is there a local county show or a carnival? What sporting events happen? Is there a local theatre or cinema? Do you have a local venue for musical events?

Once you have identified the event and gained the appropriate permission, you need your collectors and collecting materials. The requirements will be similar to those for a street collection. You may, however, want to use different devices or more collectors as you may be collecting only for short periods of time; for example it may not be popular if you try to collect during the sporting action. Remember, at big events you have large numbers of people passing collectors quite quickly, so you do not want people stopping to put money into normal hand-held collecting tins; a bucket would be far more appropriate but again, this must be sealed. Many of the specialist companies sell a bucket lid that seals the bucket and still enables donors to literally throw money in.

You also need to consider where your base will be sited and where the best places are for your collectors to be positioned. If it is a big event at which the police could be involved with crowd control, you should inform them about the collection and they may have certain requests regarding positioning of collectors.

As with most collections you need to plan well in advance to get the booking confirmed in good time. Also, again, keep the details for the future and thank everybody.

COLLECTIONS AT EVENTS SUMMARY

- research the locality
- gain the appropriate permission and check whether a licence is required
- recruit collectors
- arrange the positioning of volunteers and control base
- acquire the necessary materials
- thank everyone.

Regular giving collections

These are based on the idea of a set amount being donated and collected on a regular basis, for example a penny a day or fifty pence a month. Here you are looking for a regular commitment from both donor and collector. The collector would have a small number of people from whom to collect, probably ten to twelve. The donors would normally receive a simple brief written update on the charity on a regular basis, helping to reinforce the commitment to and interest in the charity.

The idea has been translated to work with groups (such as scouts), where each member of the group receives a small collecting box, usually a disposable one, for a period of time and deposits their regular amount; this is then collected at the end of a given period.

The regular giving idea can also be used with themes, for example every time someone swears or mentions the weather they have to make a donation. This works best in an office or family situation. Again a collecting box specifically for this purpose should be provided.

Specific item collections

As the title suggests, these are collections of particular items. There are two main types of collections:

- items that can be sold, e.g. tin foil, foreign coins, aluminum cans, used stamps, toner cartridges;
- items to be used directly, e.g. toys, clothes, food, spectacles, etc.

With the first type of collection you have to research the area carefully, as there are considerable administration implications. How are you going to turn the donated items into money? You will need to find a company prepared to take the items and give you a good price for them. You should also think about transportation, storage and sorting, all of which can incur costs.

The second type of collection is slightly easier as it has one stage less to worry about. You would still have to arrange storage and sorting facilities, however, as not all of the donated items may be of the standard you require. Items may need mending, cleaning or maintenance of some kind.

You should consider the materials you need to collect the items. The receptacle used would need to be appropriate to the item, and could be quite large. You would also need to arrange for the collection and transfer of donated items to the central storage area.

Depending on the method used to collect the items, you will need to acquire the appropriate permits. For example, if you collect house to house or in a public place you need the appropriate collections licence from the District Council.

Fund raising in educational environments

Schools

In general, children and young people can be enthusiastic fund raisers and participants in fund-raising events. Approaching them in the school environment, where they are a captive audience, is a convenient and effective way of recruiting their interest and support for your charity. The problem is that innumerable other charities will have the same thought and schools are heavily targeted for fund raising. In fact, some of the larger charities have programmes aimed exclusively at fund raising with young people. Schools are also increasingly involved in raising funds for themselves. These factors should not put you off, but they should dictate your method of approach. You should also consider the educational and community involvement aspects, which can be very important to schools.

You will probably already know of the schools in and around your area, but it is worth a bit of research to ensure you have a comprehensive list. The local telephone book will provide useful information as will locally produced directories. Lists (usually produced for parents), are available from the Local Education Authority which give not only the name, address and telephone number of the school but also the name of the head teacher and often the number of pupils in the school. If you are planning to approach a number of schools within one authority's area, you could consider sending a letter to the Director of Education's office to outline briefly your appeal and inform them of your proposal. The head teacher, however, will usually be the person to allow you access to the pupils within the school. This is therefore an important contact and should be well thought out and prepared. You may have a member of your fund-raising group who has a contact at the school or is a school governor or a member of the parent teachers association. You may have some knowledge of the school and its activities from other local contacts and research, so do gear your approach bearing in mind anything you have learnt about a particular school's policy on supporting charities. You need to have planned possible fund-raising activities to present to the head teacher, but do be flexible as they may have their own suggestions to make.

A proven way of raising money with school children is via a sponsored game, a copy of which each child can take home to complete. This could be anything from a quiz to a colouring game, depending on the age group. There are a set number of questions to answer, or items to colour in, and the child is sponsored for the number they complete correctly. You could adapt this idea to be a quiz about the locality. Remember a space should be provided for a parent or guardian to sign their consent for the child to participate. It is also a good idea to include information for parents so they know what their child has to do. Consider how something like this is going to be administered, as much time and several visits to a school can be involved. Completed games have to be marked and returned to the children with clear instructions on collecting and banking their sponsor money – ideally bringing it into the school. This can be done by a volunteer, or you can supply the school with the answers in the form of a poster to be displayed or individual answer sheets.

Remember, it is important to thank your supporters, so consider presenting the school and the children with certificates to acknowledge their support. Many charities offer other rewards for fund-raising achievements, but this is a sensitive area and should be discussed fully with the head teacher before any such idea is introduced to the children. You should ensure that any awards offered are in line with the ICFM guidelines (these are available from the ICFM) on this subject. Sponsored events can be very successful with young people, particularly as the school can usually provide an appropriate venue, e.g. school hall, playing field, etc. (*See Chapter 8.*)

Sponsorship is the best way of raising funds with school children, but there are other possibilities. Some of the methods covered in Section 5.1 work well with young people; especially the idea of individual collecting devices and specific item collections. There are also opportunities to become involved with activities that the school already runs or festivals they celebrate, such as the school play, or carol concert, the summer fête, harvest festival, Diwali etc. Many schools, particularly secondaries, have pupil charity councils who decide which charities they want to support. They will also have ideas about how they want to raise the money, so again be flexible but be prepared to offer advice and guidance.

Consider what you and your charity can offer the school. Most schools will welcome a guest speaker for assemblies – think carefully about this presentation, which needs to be pitched to the age group. It needs to contain information on your charity and how the children's contribution can help. This presentation is your opportunity to motivate the pupils to support your cause, so do make the most of it; it will also be heard by the teachers and probably the head teacher and can serve to inform them about what the pupils can do to help. Ideally you should aim to speak to fairly large groups, as becoming involved in numerous class talks can become very time consuming. Your presentation may offer the possibilities of further work in the classroom; teachers may pick up on themes you have introduced for project work. So do consider the educational content of what you have to say.

Materials produced by your charity, such as information leaflets, can be useful for project work as well as providing further information about the cause. The charity may even produce education packs specifically for schools. Make the most of what is available to you. Provide a display in the school with information on the charity and reminders about the fund-raising activity. This display is likely to be seen by parents too, and will act as a reminder for them as well as the children.

Actual charity projects locally can offer opportunities for the pupils to become directly involved with the cause. There can be nothing more motivating than seeing what your fund-raising efforts can help to achieve. Schools are interested in forming stronger links with their community, and it could be that your charity project provides this opportunity for them.

Schools may want to be involved in joint fund-raising activities where money is raised both for the school and a charity. This can be an attractive idea, but great care should be taken in the production of materials for such projects, as they must communicate the joint aspect of the fund raising clearly to any potential donor.

When working with a school, as with many areas of fund raising, you should be thinking of developing an ongoing relationship. Many schools adopt specific charities or support two or three on a regular basis. Therefore ensure that your contact with the school is an enjoyable and rewarding experience, and hopefully you will be back.

It is important to ensure that any contact you have with young people is appropriate, so do follow the ICFM guidelines when working in this area.

Further education

All further education establishments, universities, technical colleges, sixth form colleges, etc, hold a population of young people who, if they can be motivated, can be one of the most effective groups for fund raising. Whilst it is not very likely that you will be able to speak to the student body *en masse*, you will be able to access the various student committees and possibly mount some sort of display to promote your charity. Students make good volunteer collectors, especially for street and event collections, where a lack of inhibition is a definite advantage, as well as excellent participants in sponsored events. Most colleges and universities are used to fund raising for charity, usually through a rag committee.

Rags

College rags are usually very well organised, and some have a person employed specifically to oversee the activities. Considerable amounts of money can therefore be raised by rags (approximately £3 million per annum), and any approach to a rag committee needs to be carefully thought out. A local charitable project could apply to the rag for a grant, or a larger charity may want to become more actively involved: perhaps supplying resources such as collecting tins to help with fund raising. Whatever you hope to achieve, make your approach in good time, as planning takes place well in advance. Be clear about what you want and what you can offer in return.

TOP FIVE UK RAGS IN 1993/94

		£
1	Loughborough	154,101
2	Nottingham Karnival	95,000
3	MUSCA	87,972
4	Sheffield Students Charities Appeal	80,053
5	Bath Area Colleges Charities Appeal	66,156

Source: The BIBIC League Table

6

CHOOSING THE RIGHT PEOPLE

Groups and committees

At the beginning of this book I emphasised the fact that people give to people. Therefore the more people you can involve in your cause, the more you can ultimately hope to reach. You will also recall that one of the three ways people can help you is by giving you time, so you need to create vehicles through which they can do this. One of the most popular and effective ways of fund raising for a charity is to bring together a group of motivated individuals who are prepared to use their time and expertise (and in some cases money) to support a cause, but before embarking upon this course of action, ensure that the organisation's governing document does not exclude the formation of groups. Then obtain written permission for your initiative, setting out the terms and controls.

Groups are formed to meet many fund-raising objectives, and clearly the identified objective(s) will dictate the make-up of the group. They can be formed for the short, medium or long term, again dependant on their reason for being. So, what are the reasons for forming a fund-raising group? There are many, but the basic answer is to make money for the charity. You could bring together a group of people who become the local face of a national charity, or are raising funds for a locally based cause. In either case the group will meet regularly and organise a range of different fund-raising activities. Group members are replaced as they leave, ideally with someone from a similar section of the community or with similar skills. Groups may be formed for a specific activity, e.g. organising a fun day, and once this is completed they may disband. In this case the group would probably comprise some members of the main local group with other individuals co-opted in to add appropriate skills for the particular activity. A group could be formed for a specific time period, e.g. to organise events to celebrate a charity's particular anniversary. In any case, a group should be made up of individuals representing as many different appropriate sections of the community as possible, to ensure maximum access to these various sections.

Forming a local group

The starting point for forming a group has to be research; bear in mind throughout this phase exactly what you want the group for and what you want them to do. You need to compile a list of the people you want to target for your group, so you will need to know something about the community in which you will operate. It may well be that you already have a good idea of who you want as the core members of your group, or you may use the local knowledge of others to point you in the right direction. A good deal of information can be gained by reading through the local newspaper and talking to local people. Some of the people to take note of in your research and discussions could be:

- chair of: Rotary, Round Table, Ladies' Circle, Women's Institute, Soroptomists, Lions Club, etc.
- local mayor and councillors
- officials of local hobby clubs and societies
- local business people, in particular managers of local banks and building societies
- members of the local church from the minister to the church wardens and elders
- officials of the local Chamber of Commerce (you may even consider becoming a member yourself for networking purposes).

Compile as comprehensive a list as possible considering:

- people you know
- people you knew
- acquaintances
- people you know of

- people who have been recommended to you
- people highlighted by your research.

NB Networking has to be the key, if you talk to somebody and they are unable to help you, make sure they recommend someone else.

Categorise the people on your list as:

- friends
- family
- colleagues
- neighbours
- local tradespeople and business people
- churches
- clubs and societies
- media.

You will be surprised how your list will grow and develop with careful thought and increasing local knowledge. If you have colleagues working with you, get them to go through the same process. Eventually you will have a comprehensive range of prospects.

Now review the list considering:

- achieving a balanced group representing a cross-section of the community
- who might have the strongest interest in your cause
- what you know about these people
- what are the chances of gaining their active support given what you have learnt about their other commitments — pay particular attention to the other charitable causes they support and if any of these conflict with your own cause
- who do you know who could make the approach to your prime prospects for the group — sometimes you will have to rely on a cold approach but an approach from a peer or someone they know will always have a greater chance of success.

Your list will have included some names that you decide not to approach to become part of your group, do not discard them as you may want to use them for other purposes. They could be part of sub-committees formed for specific projects, they could be future donors, etc. Remember anyone on a committee should be able to *GIVE, GET* or *GET OUT*. They need to be able to donate, find other donors or find another interest; remember, perfection is not always achieved.

Once you have your group members enlisted you will need to consider the structure of the group, and whether it will operate successfully on an informal basis or needs a formal structure with appointed officers. Traditionally groups have always used officers, but with many of the new younger profile groups these are not popular and can put people off joining. On the assumption that the majority of groups will adopt officers you will now need to consider their appointment. You will need a chair, vice chair, treasurer and secretary, who should be elected by the other members of the group for a fixed term.

Chair

Clearly the most important officer, as the person who is responsible for the activities and direction of the group, in line with the objects of the organisation and the policies of its trustees. They will need to have the support of the majority of the group, and through their enthusiasm should motivate not only group members but potential supporters. While this is a responsible position, a good chair quickly learns to delegate and play to the strengths of other group members. Diplomacy and general people skills are also key to the success of this position.

Vice chair

A useful position to create in any group, in the eventuality that the chair is unable to attend a meeting or function, and should also really be considered as a back-up should the chair resign or move on. On this basis, role and qualities should be along the lines of those outlined above.

Treasurer

One of the key roles of any group, and increasingly one of the hardest roles to fill. Ideally you need somebody who deals with finances in their day to day work, failing that you should look for somebody whose numeracy and book-keeping skills can be trusted. This individual must feel comfortable with money as they will control all the income, outgoings and any other financial liabilities. They will need to keep detailed and accurate records of all transactions, and depending on the status of the group will need to prepare basic annual accounts which may be subject to audit and further scrutiny.

Secretary

The role that I would describe as the heart of any group, the secretary looks after the committee in general and keeps officers under control. Secretarial skills are useful, as is a good understanding of the English language. The secretary co-ordinates all meetings, agendas and minutes; keeps records of any members, helpers and donors; prepares any necessary literature, newsletters etc. With all of this to do, a high level of commitment is essential.

The choice for these officers, particularly for the first time, is crucial to the success of your group and will set the scene for the future so do give very careful thought to who you are going to ask to put themselves forward for these roles, especially the chair. While many committees will follow a democratic process in selecting their officers, it is as well to remember that, as the fund raiser, you should consider the relevant positions carefully and decide who you believe will fill them most effectively. Some of the quieter members of the group may need encouragement to come forward, and it is ultimately up to you to ensure the best make-up of officers.

> NB Job descriptions for the above positions will help to clarify responsibilities.

The first meeting

It is crucial to have a successful first meeting of your new group to ensure that the motivation of the members is sustained and transfers into action. Therefore, careful planning and preparation is a must.

Prior to the meeting you will have decided on the appropriate format for meetings considering the individuals who comprise the group. If you are going for the more formal route you will have already identified the people likely to fulfil the key roles and will have sounded them out on their willingness to take on the duties. So the first item of business will be to elect formally the officers of the group.

The constitution for the group will also have to be adopted. This should be a simple, common sense set of rules for the conduct of group business to which everyone concerned adheres. These rules must be in keeping with the organisation that the group represents and, if they are part of a groups network, other groups formed to support the same charity. A constitution should help and support a committee, not become a hindrance.

It is a good idea to have at least one project prepared for the group to get its teeth into, to engender a sense of purpose and direction. You also need to allow space for the creativity of the group to develop, so a balance of prepared and new suggestions should be achieved.

The venue is important too as this will help to add to the atmosphere of the first meeting. Consider including some unstructured social time, so that the individuals who make up the group can get to know each other and start to build relationships. Have sensible and realistic expectations of the first meeting. If you have elected the officers and settled the group down you will have achieved a lot.

Other types of group

Industry advisory committee

This is a group of influential business people brought together to advise the charity about how best to deal with the commercial sector and to introduce the charity to their contacts in the sector. (This type of group is covered in Chapter 9.)

Events committee

A committee brought together with the specific purpose of organising a one-off or possibly annual event. (See Chapter 8 for further information on this type of group.)

Campaign committee

This type of committee is often formed for a short period, usually to lobby for a particular campaign. They prepare and carry out a strategy for getting the ideas of a particular campaign heard and specific objectives achieved.

Publicity committee

A group of people brought together because of their expertise or interest in the area of the media and publicity in general. They could be a sub-committee of a main fund-raising group, or a committee that advises a whole charity on publicity matters.

County committee

These are often used by larger charities to create a local presence throughout the UK. Like the committee structure outlined in the main section above, they draw together key individuals on a county wide basis.

Friends of

This is a term used to cover groups affiliated to other organisations, e.g. Esher Friends of Imperial Cancer Research Fund.

———————— Volunteers ————————

Throughout this book I cover many roles that volunteers can fulfil. These are very varied and require different types of people and levels of commitment. They all have one thing in common, and that is that you are asking people to give of their time. No one can doubt the value of having a capable band of volunteers, but this does not happen without organisation and support. In this section I am going to look at ways of making the most effective use of their time.

Finding volunteers

As you get more and more people interested in your charity, the more you are going to be able to recruit by word of mouth. Each person whom you get on board will have other contacts, and this is a very effective way of finding volunteers, but do be careful not to call on 'favours' from friends and relatives to often.

Local organisations can be a good source of helpers especially for specific events, e.g. the cadets could act as marshals at an event, the Lions or Ladies' Circle could supply volunteers for a street collection. You can find details of the contact person for each organisation from lists held at the local library. Many areas have volunteer bureaux and there are specific organisations, like REACH (Retired Executives Action Clearing House) or CVS (Council of Voluntary Service), that specialise in placing volunteers.

Local advertising is another good way of finding helpers for your charity. Cards can be placed around the area — in shops, libraries, leisure centres, Citizens Advice Bureaux, community centres, etc. Advertisements can be placed in local newspapers or a letter sent to the editor for publication. Local radio stations run community service items and could include your request for volunteers. Make the most of opportunities the charity is creating. You could have a leaflet about volunteering available at other events being run, to go out with mailings etc.

I have stressed several times the importance of keeping good records of everyone approached for anything for your charity, (see the section on the Data Protection Act in Chapter 10). It may well be that, while talking to people about a different activity, someone has been recommended who will make an ideal volunteer. Therefore, it is worth going back over your records to pick out these leads.

Recruiting volunteers

You need to consider the job or jobs for which you wish to recruit your volunteers. It is a useful exercise to compile a simple job description, as this will not only be a help to potential volunteers but will also help you to clarify exactly what it is you need doing and the type of person you are looking for. Generally, volunteers respond well to job descriptions. They feel more integrated with the staff, more valued and, therefore, work better and in a more structured manner. The job description should cover:

- a brief description of the purpose of the job
- a list of the tasks to be undertaken
- detail the experience and skills that the work requires

- the time commitment that you are looking for
- any other specifics, such as expenses reimbursed, own car necessary, references required, etc.

Once you have decided on the job description and advertised the job, you need to set up interviews for the people who respond. It can be useful to get applicants to complete a brief application form to give you an idea of their past experience and skills, and to allow you to identify areas you want to explore further at interview. Decide upon a venue, which could be their home or a local office or other suitable place. List your priority requirements using the job description and plan your interview questions.

The role that the volunteer is to fulfil may be crucial to the success of your charity, so it is essential that you give yourself every opportunity to recruit the right person. Many people find it quite difficult to work with volunteers. This is because they view them differently to members of staff, but if a volunteer is to succeed they will need to undertake the same work pattern as a paid member of staff. Therefore, when you manage volunteers they should be treated in the same way as any member of staff, setting them objectives within an agreed time frame, a target and an agreed way of working.

It can be difficult to tell someone who has volunteered to give their time to a charity that they are not suitable, but the needs of the charity must come first, and much damage can be done by having the wrong person in a key role. Ideally you should be able to direct them to another volunteer role that is more appropriate to their skills.

Some volunteer roles may be low key and might only require the commitment of a few hours once a year. If this is the case it is not appropriate to go through the stages covered above. However, whatever the volunteer is doing for you they should know what is expected of them and have clear written instructions covering the task to be performed, timings, contact details, etc.

Keeping volunteers

People volunteer for many different reasons and an understanding of their motivation for volunteering is important in enabling you to keep them. Probably the main reasons are:

- interest in the cause
- time available
- want to meet people
- want to be useful and achieve something
- want influence
- the desire to be part of a group.

You therefore need to ensure that the task you give them meets their reason for volunteering. For example, if someone is keen to meet people, they need to be given a job that involves working in a team or a group.

Developing good communication channels between your volunteers and your organisation is very useful in allowing people to feel part of a team. Make sure they are up to date with the charity's achievements and objectives. This could be done via a newsletter and by ensuring they receive other relevant literature that the charity produces. Having volunteer meetings at which charity representatives can speak and volunteers can chat to each other is another good way of keeping people informed.

Volunteers need to feel that they are supported in their work so it is important that they are well trained, contacted regularly and know who to contact and how in case of a query.

In order to maintain their motivation, people need to be recognised for their achievements, and there are many effective ways of doing this, ranging from a mention in a newsletter to a presentation of a gift at a meeting. Never take anybody's support for granted, it is a sure way to lose them.

The Volunteer Centre UK organises a Volunteer Week each year which offers an opportunity to thank your volunteers and recruit more.

7

SHOPS AND MAIL ORDER

Shops and stalls

Charity shops are now a dominant force on many high streets in the UK. In some towns there can be up to 12 charity shops, all competing to secure donated goods to sell. This is done mainly with the help of an army of volunteers drawn from the local area. The growth in charity shops in the last ten years has been spectacular, with nearly 6,000 throughout the country, and this does not include those temporary shops that appear and disappear in the high street. The certainty about this growth is that, if the shops were not a viable source of funds, many charities would not continue to invest in this way.

The old image of the charity shop as an on going jumble sale has long disappeared, and charities now compete to project a warm, clean and professional image to attract regular donations and new customers. By attracting donations of second-hand goods, clothing and bric-à-brac, which are sorted and cleaned the shop is then able to market them at a reasonable price. Larger charities pay staff to manage the shop with a support staff of volunteers. If a shop is open during normal hours for six days a week, it will require a large bank of volunteers, since the average volunteer will offer to do two half day shifts and, depending on the size of the shop, you will need two or three volunteers on duty at any time. You also need to allow for sickness cover, and for last minute changes to the rota. Before opening a shop, you should review your existing volunteers and whether they are willing to become involved in trading activities, which will not suit every type of volunteer.

Much work will need to be invested in shops and it is well worth trying out this activity in a rent free site in order to test your ability to stock, market and run a local shop. To set up a temporary shop you should identify a site in your area that has become vacant, with no immediate successor tenant. Then identify the landlord through a local property agent, local knowledge or property details. The landlord may be willing to allow you temporary, rent free access on the understanding that you will pay expenses such as electricity, gas, water and rates. The landlord will require you to take out insurance cover and will want an assurance that you will vacate the premises at short notice if a paying tenant appears.

Even with a temporary shop, you must ensure that it is in a good position, with suitable passing trade; that it has good access for dropping off stock and loading; that it is in reasonably good decorative order and has at least 600 to 1,000 square feet of sales space, with further space for sorting, cleaning and staff rest breaks. If you decide to go ahead, you can compromise over some of these factors, but it is not worth settling for an inferior site as it will only waste time and energy and lessen the chance of a successful financial outcome. The property market is complex and, even when using a temporary site, it is worth seeking professional legal advice. A local agent may donate their services, or one of your existing volunteers may be able to secure this for you. Most landlords require a signed agreement and you must abide by these policies enforced by property investment companies. Charity Shop Services is an organisation that will help with pro forma agreements and negotiations with landlords.

In this area temporary can mean from one week to several years, but you must balance your investment of time and resources against the probable length of occupancy. If the operation proves to be successful, you should consider moving your rent free occupation onto a commercial leasehold basis. Then you can begin to invest small sums on the presentation and style of the shop. Large charities tend to avoid temporary shops because they want to compete for the best long-term leasehold and freehold sites. Therefore, local charities can take advantage of the short-term opportunities.

If you move into leasehold or freehold property, then professional advice is essential before negotiating and signing contracts. You will also need to assess your liabilities; can you get out of the lease without enormous financial penalties? Draw up operating budgets to include all overheads including rent, rates, insurance etc. Then you can estimate how much stock you will need to receive and sell to make a profit for the charity. Charity shops do receive rate relief, but only if they are selling mainly donated goods. Large charities are beginning to sell small amounts of new goods in their shops in order to supplement takings, but most charities are careful not to let this development affect their rate relief, which can be nearly 100 per cent of the cost, allowing for the discretionary local authority allowance. Charity shops do not have to charge VAT on sales of donated goods, but, if registered for VAT, they can claim refund of VAT paid in connection with the operation of the shop.

Making your charity shop work

- From the moment you decide to venture into this area, begin to recruit a bank of volunteers; put posters in the proposed shop window; contact all existing supporters; approach the local paper and radio station for coverage; put postcards in other shops, libraries, health centres, etc; write to local churches, be inventive in this highly competitive area.
- Make sure that the local community knows that you will need as much stock as possible, and on an on-going basis. You must be pro-active about advertising your need at every opportunity. Consider door dropping coloured sacks to encourage householders to clear out their surplus clothes and bric-à-brac. You will need a licence to do this – see 'Collections' in Chapter 5. Make clear what day you will collect their donations; leave a phone number on your sack pack just in case of difficulties and avoid using black sacks so that they will not be confused with the rubbish collection; also avoid the colours of local door step recycling schemes. Radio appeals can be very effective in generating these donations. As a rule of thumb, only 50 per cent of donated goods will be suitable for resale. As a service to your customers, you should sort all donations vigorously and avoid displaying anything too worn and unappealing. A local rag or waste merchant will pay for sack loads of unwanted waste, so even this can raise money for your cause.

- Try to make your shop bright and attractive, using light colours and strong lights to ensure that people feel that it is clean. Look at other charity shops such as those run by Oxfam and the Imperial Cancer Research Fund, where the design is simple, bright and inviting. Do not crowd your shops with rails or stock, make it easy for customers to circulate and to browse.

- Ensure that each item is priced, preferably with the date when it was put on display. This helps with regular stock rotation and if something does not sell, do not let it take up valuable selling space. Pricing can be difficult and it is best to nominate two or three of your regular volunteers as pricers to maintain consistency. Operate a fixed price system to avoid volunteers having to engage in negotiations and bartering at the till.

- Develop a system for ensuring that income is recorded in a secure manner.

- Window displays are vital to attract custom and to convey the right image for your charity. All volunteers like to have a go at this, and you should identify the volunteers who have a natural talent for this and appoint them as window dressers. Since the large high street shops employ professional window dressers, it may be worth approaching them to see if they would be willing to donate training advice to your volunteers. Form a sensible policy to cover this area.

- Do not neglect the important issue of the charity's image and presence on the high street. Ensure strong charity branding and have charity information literature available in the shop. Include posters illustrating your work, your mission statements and progress updates. Make the shops a focal point for people wishing to make a donation. When running local events, use the shop to distribute registration and sponsorship forms.

- Always remember your most important asset: volunteers. Treat them well, involve them and thank them for their vital donation of time.

Charity shops are an extremely competitive area involving much thought and planning. However, there is still plenty of room for small local initiatives such as the local hospice shops.

Stalls

There are numerous opportunities for voluntary organisations to take a stall:

- at events
- at local markets
- within shopping precincts
- at fairs, fêtes and county shows.

These can be a cost effective way of raising money and generally promoting your cause in the local community.

This type of stall can take many forms. You should consider each opportunity in terms of the general environment of the stall and the type of passing trade you can expect:

- a sale of work, items made by volunteers. If your cause seeks to help people, could the beneficiaries themselves make items for sale?
- sale of branded goods commissioned for your cause
- sale of raffle tickets. (If these are to to be undertaken at any public place, they need to be registered as Society Lotteries.)
- design a game of chance (check legality of any proposals and register as Social Lotteries if they are to be held in a public place). This could be as simple as finding a whole egg in a box filled with egg shells; or you may consider purchasing a ready-made game kit, with all the necessary components. There are several companies offering this service. Tombolas are always popular on stalls; make sure that your version stands out from the crowd.

— Mail order trading to raise funds —

by Jeremy Shaw, Smith Bundy & Partners Ltd

Why get into mail order?

Almost all major charities sell products to their supporters by mail order. Some, such as Oxfam, Barnardo's, Save the Children and WWF have large trading operations turning over millions of pounds by mail order.

Charity mail order trading is rooted in the Christmas card business. Almost every household sends cards, and there is a widespread acceptance of the idea of sending charity Christmas cards — even the smallest charity can generate sales in this way.

Charities' motivation for getting into mail order falls into four different categories:

1 Raising additional funds: this is probably the major motivation for most charities, for who there is little justification for getting involved in trading otherwise.

2 Increasing awareness: the average charity mail order customer purchases over 25 christmas cards. So if a charity can persuade 1,000 customers to buy their cards that is potentially 25,000 households to which the charity's name can be introduced. The same logic applies to pens, T-shirts, mugs and other promotional items.

3 Recruiting new supporters: some charities believe that by developing a successful mail order trading operation they will be able to introduce purchasers to the work of the organisation, and thus expand their donor base. This is rarely true; while charity donors are often willing to help further by buying goods from the charity, the 'traffic' in the other direction is frequently much less. The more successful the mail order operation is, the more it will (and should) attract people who are buying because they want the goods, not as a favour to the charity. So inevitably these people are less likely to become donors. This is not to say that mail order recruits are not excellent 'prospects' as donors, simply that no charity has built a significant donor base on the back of trading operations, whereas many have worked the trick in reverse.

4 Furthering the objectives of the organisation: for a few charities, trading is about more than simply fund raising; it is integrally bound up with what the organisation is trying to do. The British Trust for Conservation Volunteers (BTCV), for example, sell wild-flower seeds and saplings more in order to promote the planting of native plants and trees than to make money. Oxfam runs a mail order operation, with turnover in the millions, which is founded on the basis that it sells handcrafts made in developing countries: the objective here is to promote fair trade, and to provide fair employment.

As with every kind of marketing activity, it is important to be clear about the objectives, and to set clear and sensible targets. Avoid the trap of getting into trading just because other charities are doing it. The opportunities for every charity are different — for some mail order trading will make excellent sense, for others it can prove a major drain on management time for little contribution.

Legal issues

Charity law prevents charities engaging in trading directly. For this reason almost all charities set up separate trading companies (wholly owned or controlled by the charity) which covenant all their profits to the charity. This keeps trading profits and losses clearly separated from the charity accounts, and provides the usual protection of a limited liability company. An exception to this is where the charity is selling goods that directly promote the aims of the organisation — for example a book or plants in the case of BTCV. It is highly advisable to take advice from the Charity Commissioners if this is the chosen route, to ensure that their definition of 'promoting aims' is the same as yours.

Moral issues

Just as with fund-raising programmes, it behoves charities to consider the moral aspects of trading. Each organisation must make its own judgements here, but key questions are:

- Are we happy with the environmental impact of what we are doing? This relates to the kinds of merchandise being promoted, type of paper being used in promotions etc.
- Are we and our suppliers being socially responsible? Some charities have received bad publicity in the past when it has turned out that they are selling goods (usually unwittingly) produced by sweated labour, child labour or on really low piece rates.
- Is our profitability going to match our donors' expectations? If a donor sends you an order for £100 worth of goods to help the charity, what is their expectation likely to be? Few trading operations make returns of more than 20 per cent on sales, and most are half that. If your trading operation has no other objectives than to make money, but is returning 2% on sales you should ask yourself whether you can justify that to your donors.

Management issues

Mail order trading is a very different business from direct mail fund raising or from running charity shops. Before getting involved in mail order trading you should ask yourself:

- Do you have the people in your organisation with the appropriate skills?
- Can you afford to hire in experts who can help and advise you?
- How much general management time will be taken up by the activity? That represents an opportunity cost and you need to be sure that the time cannot be more profitably spent elsewhere.

Branding issues

The purchase of goods by mail order from a charity often involves a donor in a much closer relationship with the charity than conventional fund raising. If they send you a donation, you may reply with a thank you letter and information about your work. When they send you an order you will be sending back goods that may be in their household, reminding them of you, for years.

Further, if you are using a catalogue to promote your mail order goods, you should bear in mind that nearly everyone likes window-shopping. What this means is that your catalogue promotion is likely to receive more attention, on average, than a fund-raising appeal.

The upshot of this is that mail order trading has a significant impact on the *whole* of how your charity is perceived by its supporters. If you are promoting cheap and tawdry goods in this way, then it will cast one particular shadow. If you choose to promote very expensive luxury goods, that will cast another.

Charities have been slow to catch on to this issue. Many have promoted cheap and cheerful merchandise with the justification that it sells and makes money. Increasingly, though, as charities have come to realise that the fund-raising market is ever more crowded and competitive, charities are trying harder to bring their trading propositions more closely into line with the brand values of the organisation. This is easier for those such as Oxfam and RSPB, where there are trading position that are natural extensions of the charity's objectives, but even charities such as Imperial Cancer Research Fund, which have no such natural product links, are increasingly conscious of the need to match the trading proposition to donor expectations, and keep it in line with the brand values represented by the fund-raising programme.

What sells by mail order?

We have already seen that most charity trading is founded on the promotion of Christmas cards. Christmas cards do not just sell well, they tend to offer higher profit margins than conventional gifts. This is true of many paper-based products, such as calendars and diaries, and when they are specially commissioned they also have the advantage of being less open to price comparison.

Branded goods

Most charities entering the mail order field believe that goods carrying their own brand or logo will be welcomed by donors. This is not necessarily so. There are certain charity logos that people are happy to flaunt on T-shirts, mugs, pens etc., but others where this simply doesn't work. Fashionable, campaigning brands such as Greenpeace, sell this kind of merchandise with considerable success, but it doesn't take much imagination to realise that a Help The Aged T-shirt is likely to sell less than a bird-design T-shirt promoting RSPB. So before investing hundreds or thousands of pounds in branded merchandise, ask yourself whether anyone outside your own staff and volunteers would want the merchandise; better still, ask the potential customers themselves.

Mail order products

It is a fact that most people don't like to buy by mail order. In no market sector does it take more than 15 per cent of retail sales. Fortunately there is a large body of experience of mail order selling which has been built up over the years, and this can be summarised into these seven key attributes of successful mail order products:

1   Not available in retail: people will buy products that can only be bought by mail order. Sometimes this can include products which

actually are available at retail, but which perhaps don't have distribution to the kind of stores your customers or donors would visit.

2 Cheap: a bargain motivates people in mail order just as it does in most forms of marketing.

3 Tells a story: a product which comes alive through the copy, by telling a story about the way it's made or what you can use it for.

4 Organises: everybody wants to be more organised. Products that promise this, such as special storage boxes, handbags, etc, are found in nearly all mail order catalogues.

5 Personalises: personalised products sell well in catalogues for two reasons. First simply because they appeal to people, second because mail order makes it easier to present and to service this kind of business.

6 Looks good in print: some products look better in print than they do on the shelf. In print you can make the product come alive with pictures and models.

7 Promises a benefit: a classic example of this is the well known *Innovations* catalogue in the United Kingdom. Have a look at the way it is written. Every item begins not with a product description or title, but with a benefit: 'Wash windows faster', 'Transfer your old film to video'. That's the ultimate mail order rule: sell the product benefits, not the features.

Be wary of

There are some products you should think about very carefully before putting them into a mail order catalogue:

● Foodstuffs: not just because they are often perishable, but because profit margins on them tend to be low. However, well chosen foods which make good gifts can sell well (be aware of the Food Safety Act);

● Dated goods: calendars and diaries all sell well, but be careful with your sales projections, and make sure you have good margins on them. Come January, they are practically worthless;

● Clothing: this sells well by mail order, but returns can be horrendous, and 35 per cent is not uncommon. Unless you really know what you are doing, stick to loose garments like T-shirts and wrap-round skirts, and even then allow for a 5 to 10 per cent return in your profit margins.

- Fragile items: almost anything can be shipped by mail order with proper packaging, but do remember to take the cost of that packaging into account when calculating prices and profit margins.

When to sell

What's the best time to offer goods by mail order? We've already seen that Christmas cards underpin many charity offerings, so naturally the autumn season works best. Those charities that publish catalogues for both Christmas and Spring typically find they do five to ten times as much business with a Christmas catalogue.

But when should you mail your Christmas promotions? The answer is earlier than you think. Most charities mail their catalogues in July or August – if you mail later then you may be missing out, as your supporters are probably getting catalogues from several other charities too.

If you are producing a small promotional leaflet, though, it may be better to wait until September. For it is in September and October that most orders are received. A big 32 page catalogue will sit around the home for weeks until people get round to using it. If you are using a small 4 page flyer, then it will be used quickly or not at all, so mail it later.

Just as you may send reminder mailings to follow on from direct mail appeals, so it often pays to send reminder mailings to follow your mail order promotion, particularly to existing customers. Some charities mail their Christmas catalogue up to three times in this way.

Who to sell to

Just as committed supporters who are giving donations by standing orders and deeds of covenant typically prove to be the most responsive to *ad hoc* appeals, so they are typically most responsive to mail order promotions too. (Be aware of the requirements of the Data Protection Act when transferring names from a charity to a trading company.)

When beginning a trade operation, test mail to all the different segments of your donor base. Once it is up and running use the same rules as apply in other kinds of direct marketing: measure the success of each segment and mail people on the basis of their past recency of purchase, frequency of purchase and value. If they have stopped ordering, send an appropriate letter with your trading promotion asking the customer to buy again.

Mixing mail order and fund raising

While mail order can provide a useful source of potential new donors for a charity (though it should never be embarked on for this reason alone), you also need to think about whether your mail order promotion may actually damage the fund-raising revenue you get from your supporters.

There are no hard and fast rules on this. Various charities have carried out structured parallel tracking tests over the years to see whether offering mail order promotions to donors improved or degraded their propensity to give, and all have different opinions of the result. Ultimately you need to assess this for your own organisation. Key issues are:

1 If you are mailing appeals to your donors only once or twice a year, then it is easy to add an extra mail order promotion without damaging response to other appeals.
2 If you include a mail order promotion with an appeal, you will almost certainly degrade response to that appeal, and the degradation is rarely exceeded by the profits on the mail order promotion. Keep them at least four weeks apart.
3 If you are mailing appeals to donors frequently, a mail order promotion can be a way of asking them to help again, without them feeling that you are constantly asking them for money; this is a different tone of voice.
4 It never hurts to add an appeal element to a mail order promotion. At the least you will increase the value of the top-up donations you should always ask for with orders; at best you can pick up some valuable extra covenants for very little effort.

Promotional materials

We have looked at many different strategic aspects of mail order trading for charities, but what should you actually send people?

One big difference between mail order and conventional fund raising is that the cost of entry is far higher. To sell products off the page you almost always have to use colour. Colour involves special photography and more expensive printing. Colour printing economics is also quite different from the economics of one or two colour printing typically used for fund-raising appeals – it is expensive to set up, but over large volumes there is very little difference. So for example a catalogue which might cost 25p a copy to print in a quantity of 25,000 will come down to just 5p a copy if you print 2,5000,000. And that doesn't take into account the cost of photography which is fixed regardless of the number of catalogues your produce.

There is another factor which militates against small mail order operations; the larger the range of goods you offer, the more profitable it will typically be. Naturally this isn't true if you simply fill up a catalogue with goods no one wants. But generally, the more pages you have, the longer people hang on to the catalogue, the greater response and the higher the average order value. As distribution costs don't go up in direct proportion to size, a bigger catalogue is nearly always more successful than a smaller one.

Look around at the catalogues you see – not just the charity ones. You'll see many of 32 pages or more, but few of 8 pages, 12 pages etc. That's because the people who produce them know how the arithmetic works.

This doesn't make it impossible to get into mail order in a small way, and there are probably more charities in mail order in a small way than commercial companies. But it does mean that unless you have the skills, experience, resources and capital to make a big investment you should either stick to offering a small profitable range of goods to committed supporters or get the help of a firm that specialises in producing syndicated catalogues for charities.

Syndicated catalogues

The idea behind syndicated catalogues is simple. It acknowledges that small charities cannot afford to produce large lavish catalogues since they don't have the number of supporters they need to recoup the high start-up costs. So instead the same catalogue is produced for several different charities, with just the covers and order forms being changed. Companies offering this service include Barnardo

Publications, Basildon, Essex (a division of Barnado's), Webb Ivory, Burton on Trent, and Innovations Mail Order, Kingston, Surrey.

Syndicated catalogue contracts can be put together in many different ways. The choices that can be made are:

- simply changing the name on the cover
- mixing existing pages from other catalogues to create a 'new' mix
- using existing photography but a new design
- having some 'standard' pages and some pages with your own personal items such as Christmas cards and branded goods.

In contractual terms there are many choices too. You can go for a low-risk approach where the company bears all the costs and you simply receive a small percentage of the sales, through to the other end where you bear all the costs and take the profit or loss, with various stages in between. Which is best for your organisation will depend on size, resources, skills and experience. Whatever you do, think carefully and long, and research your 'partner' company fully, talking to as many of their other charity customers as possible, particularly those of a similar size to yours.

NB Syndicated catalogue providers may be regarded as commercial participators under Part II of the Charities Act 1992.

Getting people to buy

When it comes to getting people to buy from your catalogue, your objective should be to create a mail order proposition that appeals in its own right – you do not want people to buy from you out of pity, so the charity factor should be simply a bonus that gives you extra sales. Producing such catalogues is a complex subject about which whole books have been written, but here are a few key issues of relevance to charity marketers:

Photography

Next to product, good photography is the most important aspect of a catalogue. The copy is there to clinch the sale and provide the confidence to purchase. But if people are not attracted and excited by the picture, they won't get as far as the copy.

Models bring a catalogue alive, even when you are not selling clothing. But be careful what kinds of models you use. If your donor base, like most charities, is predominantly aged 55+ you will do yourself no favours letting your photographer populate it with 20-something beautiful people. On the other hand, don't go to the other extreme and use ordinary people. We are all so used to seeing models in print that when you do see real people in an advertising situation it looks bizarre, so use models, but 30-somethings and 40-somethings!

Incentives

All mail order companies use incentives to get customers to order, to increase average order values, to get second orders, etc, but you should probably not, although you need to think carefully about the psychology of purchase. You will be working hard to ensure that your trading proposition stands up in its own right, but most of your customers will believe that, at least partly, they are buying goods from you to help the cause. As a result, offering incentives to order can often reduce response. This isn't always true, there are certain kinds of charity typically appealing to younger people with more of a 'membership' feel, where incentives can work. If you are not sure where your organisation falls the answer is simple: test. It's difficult to make lots of tests in mail order catalogues since the economics of colour print could argue against it, but you can and should test things on order forms like incentives, postage and packing rates, ways of asking for donations – here it is easy and cheap to test.

Order points

We tend to talk about *mail* order, but many such companies find that nowadays they receive over half their orders by telephone. Charity supporters, being older, tend to order by phone less often than some market segments, but 30 to 40 per cent is not uncommon. Phone ordering should be encouraged since it provides you with the advantage that if an item is out of stock a customer can be told straight away and given the chance to order something else, and you can also persuade customers to increase their order value by mentioning popular items they have not ordered. (Reference should be made to the ICFM Code of Practice on Outbound Telephone Support.)

The back end

More mail order companies have failed through poor management of the 'back end' than through poor marketing. Back end is a term mail order people use to refer to the whole business management process from the point of order receipt.

These are the key issues:

- The quicker you process a customer order, the more chance you will have of getting another order from them. This is particularly important with Christmas promotions.
- If you budget to make a perfectly respectable profit on turnover and end up refunding 10 per cent of order values through stock-outs or quality problems you won't make a penny.
- Equally, if you end up with large volumes of left over stock, you may well have to sell it at a loss. Remember your accountants will make you value it at the lower of 'cost or realisable value' – if you have to sell a stock jobber, you'll find realisable value may be less than half of what you paid. Try to negotiate 'call-off' deals with suppliers, where they reserve say 1,000 items for you, but you only commit yourself to 150 initially, calling off the balance if you need them. Only invest heavily in items like Christmas cards where you can achieve much higher margins for larger quantities and those which can be sold again the following year in mixed selections.
- Keep on top of customer service. If customer queries aren't handled promptly and efficiently they quickly spiral out of control and a simple delayed item can turn into a nightmare of confusion. Not only will you end up wasting a lot of expensive staff time, but you could lose a valuable donor in the process.
- Keep the numbers tight. All mail order companies operate rigid cost controls — they will spend what it takes to excite the customer to order and keep them loyal, but internally they are some of the tightest and most efficiently run companies you will find. If you are going to compete with them, you have to match them.

Summary

If this brief guide to mail order trading for charities has put you off, then don't be disheartened by that. The truth is that mail order is hard work, it is tough, and it does demand a whole new set of skills.

For the great majority of charities mail order trading profits fall into the 'useful' rather than 'vital' category. That doesn't mean that mail order is not worth getting into, but it does mean that you should be clear in your objectives and put together a mail order proposition that you are confident will further the public perception of your charity, not work against it.

8

ORGANISING EVENTS

There are few people who have not been to a charity event of some kind. They are extremely popular ways of raising funds as they can be enormous fun as well as profitable for the charity.

Research

Putting on any kind of event from scratch requires considerable planning and organisation. The further in advance things can be started, the more likely the project is to be a success. You also need to do some research on the event to decide the answers to the questions *why*, *what*, *where*, and *when*.

The first thing to consider is *why* you are putting your event on. Whilst this book is about fund raising, there are several reasons for having an event. You could put it on to promote good public relations. Perhaps the charity needs to increase the public's awareness of it or you want to entertain people who have helped and been involved with the project or cause. You could be looking at a recruitment exercise. Perhaps you need local volunteers to help with the project or to start up a new branch for your charity.

Be clear from the outset what it is you want to achieve from your event as this will dictate many factors in the planning and organisation. Afterwards you will want to analyse its success against your primary objective for putting it on, so you need to know what this is. The most likely reason is that you want to raise funds. Before you embark upon the planning, however, you must also do some research: what event is most appropriate for your charity, what activities are popular locally, and what sort of occasions do people want to take part in. To find out, you could:

- scour the local newspapers, even telephone the newspaper offices to ask for information. They may publish an annual calendar of events
- visit the library. They will have an events board and may hold further leaflets, flyers or sponsor forms for events advertised
- visit the local community centre, leisure centre, sports clubs etc. They will also have information boards and again you may be able to pick up further information and literature on the events
- talk to people who have organised events locally
- look at national magazines for specific activities. Many publish annual calendars of events
- market intelligence should always be the starting point but then do not be afraid to be creative
- with your fellow fund raisers or volunteers brainstorm ideas for events – be a leader not a follower.

To decide *where* you are going to hold your event:

- look at what other event organisers have used;
- consider the accessibility of the venue;
- look at the facilities available – are they appropriate?
- talk to local people – do a little market research;
- research the connections that people in your own charity or fund-raising group may have. This is often where access to the unique and non-commercial may come from;
- if your research identifies a local stately home as the most attractive and profitable venue then remember that your charitable status should give you a unique hearing when approaching the owners of such a venue.

Finally you need to do some research as to *when* is the most appropriate date for your event. You will need to:

- avoid other established local events and major national or international events in the same field;
- consider the importance of the weather to the success of your event;
- choose the day of the week that is likely to be the most popular and convenient for your target group;
- think about popular holiday weeks and any particular local holidays;
- always set the date to appeal to your customers not your committee, local dignitaries or celebrities.

There is a huge variety of events that can be organised to raise funds but all of them fall into one or more of four categories:

- *Sponsored*: where people are sponsored by individuals to participate in an activity;
- *Ticket*: where people pay an entry fee or buy a ticket to attend an event;
- *Sale*: where people attend an event to buy items;
- *Integrated*: these campaigns are based on a theme around which many different types of event and media support are organised.

Remember these categories of event are not mutually exclusive and often an event will include more than one element.

Sponsored

This is probably the most popular type of fund-raising event, offering as it does a chance for people to get involved in an activity and be sponsored for their participation. Importantly it also offers the opportunity for a much wider audience to become involved as sponsors. Almost anything you can think of can be sponsored – from swimming to singing and abseiling to aerobics. The key thing is to choose an activity that is appropriate to the group(s) you are targeting. It must be something that is popular and for which there is a good venue in the area. Take all possible precautions to ensure that any activity is run to maximum safety standards; never put participants at unnecessary risk. There are several possible reasons for someone to take part in a sponsored event – they find the activity attractive, they want to support the cause, someone asked them, some of their friends are participating, etc.

The art of getting people's early interest in your event is the key to success, as this will give them sufficient time prior to the event to seek their all-important sponsors, so contrive as many ways of getting to as many different groups as possible. It can be done in person by attending group meetings to talk about the event and the cause; this gives you the opportunity to put your case and to use your enthusiasm to motivate others. You can speak to potential participants (and sponsors) through the media (*see Chapter 12*). You could look at mailing information to appropriate local groups or individuals; details of groups can be found in specialist directories for each activity, local libraries or citizens advice bureaux. Mailing individuals is a much harder task, but clubs or magazines may include details of your event within their own mailing.

Your publicity materials should be as interesting and exciting as possible. If you have any special attractions tell people; is there a celebrity attending, is there a display being put on, are you having a prize draw? You should aim for good coverage of the area of the event and its surrounds, especially in places where similar activities are held. Make sure people have the information they need and know where to go for more, i.e. always include a contact point, preferably a telephone number, on publicity materials. The sponsor form provides opportunities for further information to be put over. You can include something about the cause; show people how their contributions can help, e.g. £20.00 can buy..., etc. Think about the colours to be used for your printed materials. Make sure they are eye-catching and attractive, clear and legible. Remember all materials should include the registered charity information and a contact point.

Consider using fund-raising awards; certificates or medals for all sponsored participants. T-shirts for people raising a specific amount, a star prize (donated by a local company) for the top fund raisier, etc. Always put a time limit on awards as it encourages prompt banking of the sponsor money, and you do not want someone claiming the top fund raiser's prize three months after you have presented it to someone else.

Banking is ultimately the most important administrative task for sponsored events. People are used to sponsorship and will often bring their money to the event, so ensure that you have banking facilities available. The more normal method is for individuals to collect their sponsorship after the event, so you need to supply them with very clear banking details and the address to which their cheques should be sent; or a telephone number for credit card payments. You will then need a system that ensures you chase sponsorship money after three weeks with a reminder letter; some people may need a second reminder, which I would recommend at six weeks.

It is likely that you will want to repeat the event, so do keep all the appropriate information – the participants, the volunteers, the suppliers, the sponsors, etc. Every time you run such an occasion you will want to learn from your successes and failures, so you should adopt the practice of writing up a complete review after each event, and being honest with yourself and your charity as to the final budgets, what did and did not work, etc.

Ticket

The key question here is 'Will enough people pay the price you are asking to attend your event?' Pricing is very important and you must be able to offer sufficient value for money. Research other events in the area that are similar to your own – how successful were they? what were they offering? how much did they charge? All the evidence suggests that people will pay to attend a charity event, but they must want to attend for its own sake. Good charity occasions are good in their own right.

As with a sponsored event, choose an appropriate activity and an attractive venue. As a charity you may be able to offer aspects that commercial enterprises cannot, e.g. you may be able to hold a concert or ball in a stately home not usually open to the public if the owner supports your cause. Involve as many people as possible in as diverse areas as possible in the selling of tickets. It is a good idea to set up a *ticket selling committee*; this may include people already associated with your charity or more likely people who are particularly interested in the event you are organising. At a very early stage this committee should formulate a full marketing stategy which looks at who the event will appeal to, where these people are and an action plan of how the committee is going to reach them. Ticket events can be one of the hardest areas to work in, particularly when you may be exposed for organisational costs. Therefore, pre-selling tickets must be your priority. Again, people will buy tickets for many different reasons, so ensure they know about the event and have been asked to attend.

Publicise widely and appropriately. As covered in the previous section, there are many ways of doing this – make the most of them. Make the tickets and other materials appropriate, e.g. if you are putting on a traditional black tie ball do not print the tickets on fluorescent card.

Sale

Here there are two equally important factors; getting enough items of the right quality to sell and attracting enough people to buy.

You will need the involvement and support of a good number of people in the collection of items for sale, if you are doing this in a public place or door to door, you will need the appropriate licence. Again publicity is important so that people know about the event and what it is you want donated for your sale. They must know how to get any queries answered and how to get any donations to you – use all your publicity materials to do this. Remember donors may also be buyers.

There is a huge variety of things that can be sold ranging from jumble to promises. There are several ways to sell any item and you should consider which is going to be the most profitable way for the type of items you have been donated and the type of people who are going to buy. Auctions, in the right setting, can generate two or three times the income of a set price sale; silent auctions can be useful at art exhibitions where people submit their bid on paper in a sealed envelope, the work of art going to the highest bidder. At society functions donors often participate in a silent auction by submitting a cheque with any bid, yet the work of art still only goes to the highest bidder, the other participants being left with the warm feeling of supporting a charitable cause! These examples illustrate that even in the straightforward area of sales there are many creative options available. Choose your venue carefully and make sure the event is suitable to the area.

While it is usual for all of your items to be donated for the different types of sales, you may also consider the growing popularity in 'Dutch sales', where people will submit more valuable items on the basis of receiving back 50 per cent or similar of the proceeds. However, you should review the possible VAT implications of such activities.

Integrated

This is the newest form of event activity, and can usually be witnessed via one of the media charity campaigns or the campaigns of some of the larger charities. It is where events from several different categories are organised under a promotional umbrella theme, e.g. Comic Relief, Children's Society Jester Appeal, Imperial Cancer Research Funds Hands On Appeal, Telethon. This is a reasonably advanced technique that usually requires considerable resources.

Resources

Event committee

You will probably find the most effective way of organising an event is to form an event committee. The balance of the committee is crucial to its success; ensure that you have a mix of the skills, experience and contacts required and that everyone is clear about their role and responsibilities. The group will probably be made up of a mixture of some of your usual charity supporters and other people brought in for their specialist skills and interests.

Volunteers and staffing

What level of manpower do you need to run the event? What skills and experience do you need to access? Start with your committee or fund-raising group – between you there will be a surprising number of contacts, so get people to list them for now and for future reference. Contact previous volunteers. Consider local organisations – cadets, sports clubs, etc. – they may be able to marshall your event.

It is vitally important to have enough helpers. Draw up a detailed plan of how many people you need and what they will be required to do. Devise a system for passing this information to each helper. If it is possible, a full volunteer briefing prior to the day is a useful exercise in uniting people and making sure that everybody knows what they have to do. If this is not possible get your volunteers to come early on the day of the event for such a briefing; either way ensure every event has a detailed manpower schedule which tells people when and where they are required and for what. It is always useful to have a couple of volunteers who have less specific tasks so that you can use them in an emergency, but do take care that they do not feel at a loose end.

Care of your volunteers and staff is just as important as care of your customers, therefore build breaks into their work schedule, ensure they have suitable catering facilities, check their transportation to and from the event, give a clear finish time and always say thank you.

There are consultants who specialise in event organisation and who will be able to offer much valuable advice and expertise. However, you should balance the cost of employing the consultant with the likely income from the event. Information on choosing and employing a consultant is covered in Chapter 17.

Budgets

How much is the event going to cost to put on? Consider every possible expense that could be incurred. Get as much information as possible and list it all down. Obviously you will try to get as much as possible donated or at a reduced cost – remember you never know until you ask – but do not assume this in your initial budget calculations unless you have had a cost or a donation confirmed. Prepare a best, worst and likely scenario. How much is the event likely to raise? Consider the capacity of the venue and the numbers similar events have attracted. What have you decided to charge for the event or what is the sponsorship per head you expect? Is there any way you can judge the likely numbers that will attend? Could participants pre-register? Could you offer a discount for pre-purchased tickets? What is the break even point? How many people need to buy a ticket before you are into a profit situation? How many participants raising the estimated average sponsorship need to be attracted?

All of the above information needs to be reviewed, on a proper operating budget sheet that details income in one column and expenditure in another, giving you a likely profit scenario. Always be pessimistic in this exercise. (See Appendix IV Part 2 for Event Feasibility Form.)

Sponsors

- Can the event run without a sponsor?
- Have you sold the event to a sponsor?
- Does the viability of the event depend on the involvement of a sponsor?

Clearly having a sponsor backing the event will make it even more profitable and can allow you to develop it further. However, a sponsor will be looking for value for their money, so it is important to have thought this through and to be prepared to highlight the benefits. As well as the considerable work involved in securing sponsors you should also consider how you might care for them at your event, where it will be your responsibility to ensure they and their guests are happy and that you deliver the package you sold them. If you secure a sponsor, you will in effect be trading, as you are selling commercial benefits, and this should be dealt with by a trading company. Simply acknowledging a sponsor can be accepted by the charity. (For more information on sponsorship see Chapter 9).

There is no VAT charge on one-off charitable fund-raising events. But, regular charity events can be liable for VAT. (See Chapter 14 for information on VAT).

Materials

You are likely to need tickets, sponsor forms, posters, information leaflets etc., and all such materials should be appropriate to your event. Therefore consider carefully your target audience – the look materials for a classical concert should be very different from those for a sponsored work out. Ideally you should involve someone with some design experience; also look at the materials you have gathered during your research, since they may provide you with some guidelines on what to do and what not to do. With the growing sophistication of home computers, you may find an enthusiast through your charity or committee who can help you design through a desk top publishing system (DTP). One of the most useful gifts in kind towards your event could be from a local design company, who for some publicity may take on designing and maybe even printing materials for an event; it is always worth asking.

Think about the colours to be used and the size and amount of text to be included – you want to attract attention but you also need them to be easily read (this is especially true for posters). Are any of the materials to be sponsored or is there an event sponsor to be considered? If there is they will need to be included in the design stage to some extent.

What needs to be included? The obvious things are the where, when and what facts of the event. You should also consider how people enter, get tickets or sponsor forms, get more information, etc. Are there any special attractions, prizes or fund-raising awards you should mention that will make the event more attractive? Do any instructions need to be included? For example 'free entry to prize draw with completed sponsor form'.

Remember that all materials must bear the registered charity information.

Publicity

This is vital. Use all the resources available to you. Involve all committee members, regular volunteers and supporters in selling tickets, distributing sponsor forms, placing posters, etc. Place information and forms in locations where they are likely to be seen by people who are going to be interested in your event. Visit libraries, community centres, leisure clubs, schools, colleges, sports clubs, theatres, concert halls, local shops, etc, and revisit them to check the condition of your posters and to ensure that they have not run out of sponsor forms, etc. Ask organisers of other local events to hand out your publicity materials at their event – you could reciprocate.

Talk to your local media. Prepare press releases for the local newspapers, radio, television, and follow them up with a telephone call. Find out the name of the person to talk to and to whom you should send your release, and keep them informed. With more unusual events you may be able to arrange a photo-call prior to the event to gain publicity, local newspapers are always on the look out for good photos. Specialist media are also worth approaching well in advance of your event, they may include a feature or an interview.

Are you prepared to pay for advertising? Where and when is most effective? Can you get it free? Do not forget publicity on the day to keep your charity high profile and to build a reputation for successful events. (See PR section for further details)

Checklists

LEGALITIES

Before organising your event make sure you know what is required in the way of permits and permissions:-

- Do you need an entertainments or liquor licence?
- Do you need any special permits?
- Are you covered by the appropriate insurances?
- Do you need first aid cover?
- Have you involved the police in you plans?

BEFORE THE EVENT

- Form your event committee
- Decide why you are putting on the event
- Do your research
- Decide on the event, venue and date
- Secure your sponsor – if appropriate
- Review your resources – do you have what is required?
- Arrange all bookings, permits, licences etc.
- Order your printing and other materials
- Maximise your publicity

ON THE DAY

- Arrive in good time
- Ensure all volunteers/staff know what their duties are
- Check the registration site/entrance is set up and manned
- All sites must be clearly signed and well set up
- Ensure everything is tidied away at the end

AFTER THE EVENT

- Thank everyone concerned
- Make sure all participants know what to do with the money they collect
- Maximise the publicity
- Evaluate the event

– Further ways to benefit from events –

Add ons

If you have gone to considerable time and trouble organising an event do make the most of it by adding other fund raising activities to it. You can run a collection or raffle or side events without it affecting the main event. In fact other activities can enhance your event and will mean you will raise more money for your charity. Make the most of all opportunities.

Repeat events

Once you have organised an event you will probably want to do it again – or something similar – and it will be much easier on subsequent occasions because of your experience and contacts. For this reason it is important to keep good records of everything that happened; what did not work as well as what did? Involve as many of the same people as possible – they too will have a greater understanding and appreciation of what is needed. Make sure everybody is properly thanked and that all loose ends are tied up because if you want to go back to them you should have left them in the right frame of mind.

People who came to your first event and enjoyed it are likely to come again and this time they may well bring friends. An annual event can become an established part of the local calendar.

It may be that someone else in your fund-raising group or committee may take on the leading role in organising a future event, so do make sure that you keep all the information in a transferable form.

Piggy-backing

This is where you become involved with an event that is already happening. You will need to research the local events to know what activities are planned. Is there a county show at which you could have a stall and/or collection? Is there a sporting event at which you could organise a side event, a collection, etc? You will need to consider how you could become involved and why the organisers would want to involve you. This is a very attractive area of events for charities as you do not have the expense or risk of organising an event from scratch. Look at local, regional and national events and brainstorm within the team for new dimensions to these events, e.g. galas, openings, new hospitality opportunities, etc.

Events are constantly being organised all over the country, so why not ask if your charity can benefit from some of them? Perhaps the local theatre will give you the proceeds of one performance, or a local sporting club will give you a percentage of their gate money? Your charity could benefit from the proceeds of a raffle organised at a company's Christmas party, etc. You will never know unless you ask. Even if an event cannot support you financially, they may be prepared to publicise an event you are organising or allow you space for a display on your charity.

9
CORPORATE FUND RAISING

Industry has a tradition of supporting charities. While this tradition has continued and developed into the twentieth century, it has changed dramatically over the last two decades. There has been a move away from traditional philanthropic giving to a much wider area of relationship and partnership fund raising, where charities and companies work together for mutual benefit. Each party can measure the benefit of their involvement in a particular project. Cash donations to charity now account for only 50 per cent of corporate funding of the charitable sector. The other 50 per cent is made up of a very large and varied range of activities. The corporate fund raising that we see nowadays is relatively new and all sides of the equation are learning how to refine it further for mutual benefit.

The company as a resource

Successful corporate fund raising relies on the ability to apply the basic fund-raising principles to companies, i.e. being able to persuade people to give you what you want, when and where you want it for the purpose you have identified. When people think of companies, they immediately imagine an insurmountable brick wall, yet companies consist of three key elements: people, budgets and resources. When you break these down, you can begin to develop effective strategies and access points into a company. For many years now, I have trained corporate fund raisers on the basis of an approach called 'The Company as a Resource'. This asks the fund raiser to take the widest possible perspective of a company, to consider time and gifts in kind

Company access points

Charity opportunities

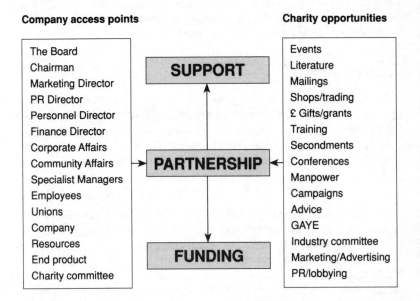

The Board		Events
Chairman	**SUPPORT**	Literature
Marketing Director		Mailings
PR Director		Shops/trading
Personnel Director		£ Gifts/grants
Finance Director		Training
Corporate Affairs		Secondments
Community Affairs	**PARTNERSHIP**	Conferences
Specialist Managers		Manpower
Employees		Campaigns
Unions		Advice
Company		GAYE
Resources		Industry committee
End product	**FUNDING**	Marketing/Advertising
Charity committee		PR/lobbying

Figure 6 The company as a resource

as well as money. By doing this, whether you are a large, national charity or a local cause with only one or two staff, you will be able to draw up a list of ways of accessing a company with suitable propositions.

Any company is multi-faceted and the easiest way to break it down is to look at the key personnel, their responsibilities and ways that they may be able to help your charity.

The board

The group of people at the top of the company; directors who are appointed to govern the company's affairs to ensure that it complies with all legal requirements and makes the largest profits for the shareholders. The chances are that your organisation may well know individual board members, they may be your trustees. They can provide the organisation with an introduction to the company, sending requests to a particular director or department, introducing the organisation and what it can do for the company. Caution is needed when using such contacts; they should be used as an introduction and not as an influence on company decisions. As with all fund raising, researching people associated with the organisation may bring some surprises and will certainly give you a bank of contacts.

The chair

The person who runs the company at the very top, and the initial target for many charities. Chairs are traditionally associated with charitable giving. They are targeted to establish their interests and enthusiasms for charitable causes, and to recruit their personal and company wealth and influence for charity committees. This approach is still relevant today and successful capital campaigns are widely publicised because of the high level of funds they generate. (*See Chapter 11*).

The chair holds the key to the company, since he or she can access every part of it. As individuals, chairs can be motivated to support causes and, once they have identified the two or three causes they wish to support, they can do much more than merely give a single donation. Many charities now put together Industry Advisory Committees, bringing together chairs from various sectors of industry.

Industry advisory committee

As a body, these committees can influence other key industrialists and support your ventures into the corporate field. They meet two or three times a year to review approaches the charity is making to industry and to advise them on the appropriateness of these approaches. Members of the committee may facilitate introductions to companies within their sector or to the right department in their own company.

If a chair of a company wishes to support your organisation, you should consider carefully whether you are going to ask for a cash donation or whether you are going to take a longer-term view and consider how their on-going association with you could open doors and give you other leads to industry.

Marketing director

Next to the chair, the individual running this department is the second most popular option for charities to approach. This is usually because charities believe they have large budgets and can, therefore, be of potentially greater value to a charity. Often if charities do not succeed when approaching the marketing department, it is simply because they forget the definition of marketing and the reason why the department exists. The Chartered Institute of Marketing defines marketing as 'The management process responsible for identifying and satisfying customer needs profitably.' Therefore, the simple rule of thumb is that any proposition should meet this requirement. Indeed, it should go further since the charity must gain some understanding of the company's business and tailor any proposals to the company. There are many ways that charities can help a company to market its products and services, but it is essential to understand how the company works and, in particular, the problems faced by the marketing department.

The two salient areas for the marketing director in terms of fund-raising proposals are sponsorship and promotions; two of the most popular forms of corporate fund raising. Both disciplines have become accepted parts of the marketing mix and have established a common language between the marketing department and the charity. For the fund raiser, they are rather complex and require a reasonably high level of understanding of the technicalities involved.

Many charities talk of sponsorship without truly understanding its meaning and they are applying the term to philanthropic support. Promotions are a difficult area to target and the majority of large, successful promotions with charities are initiated by the company. However an alert organisation within the market can put together proposals for consideration by the company.

To sell a proposal to the marketing department, you need to put yourself in the place of the marketing team and go through the processes they will go through when trying to market their product, or to position it within the market place. Your organisation appeals to a target audience and in some cases this can be a very narrow target area, but in others it is much wider. If your charity, which has the ability to attract supporters, becomes linked with a product, it will attract supporters to that product and the association should prove to be a commercial proposition for the company as well as a source of funds for the charity. You should also consider the appeal of the events and activities created by the charity in order to raise funds. These are also of interest to the company and its marketing team, who may be interested in reaching the target audience at which the events are aimed.

Public relations

This area often comes under the marketing director within the corporate structure as a discipline within the marketing mix, but can also be a department in its own right. Either way, you will find that it has funds available to fulfil the important role of promoting the company within the community and even worldwide, and monitoring problems of bad press, controversial activities, etc, that the company may face. In this department we find the true beginnings of charity sponsorship. A few years ago companies realised that, rather than just sending money, they could ask a charity representative or local dignitary to accept a cheque at a public ceremony. In addition to furnishing copy for in-house publications for circulation to customers and employees, this also provided good local and national publicity for the company and public goodwill towards the company. The mutual benefits for charities and companies were relatively basic at this stage. The relevance of charity involvement to the PR department is clearer than elsewhere and, therefore, virtually all charities target PR directors saying 'We are a great PR story. Why not support us?'

To access this area successfully, the charity should do its homework: Why should the company wish to gain a high profile through your charity? What is unique about your proposition? Is your proposition good value for money? This is the professional approach to designing proposals for a PR department in order to gain a PR opportunity.

Many companies use an external PR agency and it is worth approaching these agencies with proposals. This enables you to gauge how the agency has been briefed by the company and how you may be able to make the charity an element of that brief. For smaller, local charities, the PR department can be a useful target since they are often looking for opportunities at a local level.

Corporate affairs

This is usually closely aligned to the chair's office and is responsible for relationships with any groups influencing the success or failure of the company's activities. This team will also look at the strategic planning for the company, the corporate identity, the public's perception of the company and its rating by competitors and the government. This area, which has quite valuable budgets, is accessed by understanding what the team is trying to achieve and how it is succeeding in its aims. Charities are often in a privileged and unique position because they access many of these key groups when seeking support for their cause. By researching the charity's means of access to the groups, it may be possible to discover how this can be widened to companies. Charities are often involved in events that would be ideal vehicles to attract key decision makers, and these are the important targets for corporate affairs departments.

Corporate affairs departments can also help to lobby key groups and individuals. Therefore, you could consider how this area can help you to achieve the charity's objectives.

Personnel departments

A neglected area until the advent of payroll giving, when there was a rush of charities trying to target this department and solicit employees' support for their schemes. Personnel departments afford further opportunities for charitable involvement by allowing access to secondment, employee fund raising, social clubs, training facilities and trade unions.

There is often a formal link between the charity committee and the personnel department. In a recent survey, personnel directors expressed surprise at the lack of imagination shown by most charities when approaching their departments. Ninety per cent of charities simply looked for payroll giving and a chance to canvass the employees. Many would have had more success if they had developed a creative approach, asking for places on employee training courses run by the company, or secondment of staff to fulfil a specific need within the charity.

In the early 1990s, secondment faded into the background, but recent activities have demonstrated that it is back on the personnel director's agenda as a real possibility for consideration. Companies spend millions of pounds each year on the best training programmes for their personnel, and it is easy for them to create additional places for delegates from charities. Apart from the nominal cost of accommodation on a training course, one or two additional delegates do not register in terms of the high costs of tutorial fees.

Trade unions may not be a direct source of funding, although they do have small charitable funds available for specific purposes, but they can be a major influence when soliciting support from company employees.

A company's personnel department will know who the union representatives are and can introduce you to them to see whether the employees can be motivated from the shop floor.

Most companies have a variety of social clubs and some have social and sporting facilities. Employees are nominated to run these facilities and the personnel department is the means of gaining introductions to the social committee. Social committees can be a driving force behind large employee fund-raising initiatives, and can also generate funds in their own right. A company may have adopted a specific charity for a year, but, within the social club, they will run events, raffles and collections for other local causes. In the early days of payroll giving, the not-for-profit sector talked of the infamous company mole or insider who is sufficiently motivated to encourage their colleagues into raising funds for the cause. The social club is certainly the place to look for such people, since they will already be involved in organising activities, and they will be easily identified.

This analysis of the departments common to all large organisations can be applied to sales directors, finance directors and other specialist managers, but they may be peculiar to one company, so I have not included them in this general review of opportunities for charities. It is important not to discount them, however, as there are imaginative ways of working with them and their departments. Remember, if you can attract the support of these executives, they are the means to securing corporate support.

So far the focus has been on the heart of the company, the head office. It is now important to look at the company structure. For example:

- How is the field force organised?
- Do they have sales representatives?
- Do they have regional offices?
- Are people working from home?
- What are the resources in the field?
- What are your resources and how could they match?

Several of the company divisions already mentioned may have regional budgets in addition to their central budget. This enables them to delegate authority at ground level and a small charity may be able to gain support via local outlets. Larger organisations should be motivating regional staff to access these local budgets and resources, using the broader, head office approach outlined earlier. Trying to get a foot in the door and forging a link with a large company can offer the ideal opportunity to tap their direct lines of communication to the company centre with its larger budgets and key decision makers. Many companies are actively developing the policy of allowing their regional units to direct local philanthropic giving to a link or affinity within the local community. They also ask regional staff to express their preferences on which charitable projects to support. By working through the local offices, it is possible to build up the credibility needed to pave the way for any approach. A word of caution here; if you are operating with regional fund raisers in addition to those at head office, ensure a clear method of communication so no confusion occurs between different parts of the company. Some charities have been blacklisted by a company for creating a confusing and conflicting picture of the type of support they are seeking. This is true of the whole company resource model where different means of approaching companies have been investigated.

Now to focus on the resources available to charities. you can look at the company's end product and how this could be used in the work of the charity or as a way of raising funds. A hospice appeal may require £12,000 worth of furniture and equipment, and the best way of securing this might be to approach the suppliers of such equipment, offering a mutually beneficial package where the hospice will market the company's product to donors. A national lottery run by a charity could seek prizes from companies, in return for incorporating the corporate branding on lottery tickets, posters and publicity. Another profitable area for charities is that of obtaining company seconds or ends of lines to stock charity shops. As companies change their colours and identities, charities are finding it profitable to look for out of date staff uniforms and equipment. A creative look at the company product is very important and all offers of help should be positively reviewed. Once the charity becomes known, companies may initiate the contact by calling in with generous donations of products. The products may not be exactly what is required and it may be difficult to accept some of the offers, but if they are used successfully, the company will be sympathetic to other requests from the charity. Resource transfer is an established area in the US and a growth area in the United Kingdom.

Companies can make their facilities available to a voluntary body. Head offices and regional offices may be used for meeting venues; canteens and conference facilities are also valuable assets. Access to a company's print department with photocopiers and duplicators could be extremely helpful since the company has already included them in its budget and may agree to write off your use of the facilities. This is an easy way for the company to support the charity, since these are normal business budgets already accounted for and they will not necessarily appear against the support for the charity. It is important to be aware of the time that may be spent in securing this type of support and the value to be gained from it. For small, regionally based causes in particular, this can be useful, and local branches, local groups and volunteers should be encouraged to be alert to any such opportunities. Office stationery supplies, again written off by companies, can sometimes be provided on a supply and demand basis making your fund-raising operation more cost effective.

Charity committees and trusts

This is a well known opportunity for charities, but even here things are changing as companies feel the pressure on whatever charitable funds they have available. Most of the large corporate givers now have an established policy for selecting which causes to support. Although this part of the company exists to give away a certain amount of the company's profits, it is necessary to understand how the company wishes to dispose of its charity funds and your approach should be carefully tailored. There are some useful directories, and some companies publish guidelines. Even a telephone call to the person running this department can save much time and unsuitable approaches. Some charities still believe that the best way to gain access to philanthropic funds is to list five hundred top companies and send a circular letter to all of them. This does an enormous disservice to the sector as a whole. Successful approaches need to be well considered and well targeted in order to gain a fair hearing. So, even in this traditional corporate fund-raising area, charities need to adjust their thinking and approach and learn to communicate with the company before asking for a share of its profits.

Company agencies

Although not strictly part of the company structure, these are another important part of the company as a resource since companies rely on agencies to fulfil a variety of functions: advertising; direct mail; sponsorship; sales promotions; public relations and recruitment. The charity may find that, when a suitable proposal has been developed for a company, one of the best approaches is to contact the agency, who can advise on whether their proposal will appeal to the company, or whether it is relevant and well-targeted. Marketing and PR agencies are briefed to look for ideas to solve particular marketing or corporate problems, and so they should be receptive to a letter from the charity or to a telephone call. If an agency likes the proposal, it may consider putting some additional time into fine tuning them for presentation to the company. The proposal may, in this case, become the agency's brain child, but if the charity achieves its objectives, this is a fact of life worth accepting gracefully.

Auditing your organisation

After reviewing the points of access to the company, you need to define your organisation's market stall of opportunities. Audit your organisation to discover what you can offer a company and to define what is required from companies. Once this line of thinking has begun, it is easier to make a fairly long list of opportunities. Whether one fund raiser is responsible for all fund raising, or there is a dedicated corporate fund raiser, this particular form of fund raising is pro-active in its own right – as well as providing a service to the whole charity by marketing the activities of other departments to a company for corporate consideration. Beginning with the cause the charity supports and the projects it undertakes, these can be packaged in such a way as to attract company interest. By reviewing the charity's operations, it is possible to discover which could be helped by company support. The nature of the charity's PR, information and campaigning activities produce opportunities for corporate involvement. It is only a matter of defining them. Figure 6 on page 87, illustrates the model of the company as a resource so that the opportunities can be prioritised against the needs of the charity. Once this is completed, the objective is to bring together one or more components from each side of the equation to create a partnership resulting in funding or support. Support can be quite as valuable as funding in the long term.

Definition of techniques in corporate fund raising

Corporate fund raising encompasses a multitude of techniques and, as a result, there is considerable misunderstanding about the definitions of the various techniques. Each of the following is only a suggested definition.

Sponsorship (*See also 'Company sponsorship'*)

A two way *commercial* agreement benefiting both organisations. A sponsorship may involve more than one sponsor, in which case the definition would be expanded to encompass this.

Promotions (*See also 'Sales promotions'*)

1 Sales promotion is an immediate or delayed incentive to purchase, expressed in cash or in kind. It has a temporary or short term duration, but can affect brand images in the longer term.
2 Affinity promotion is where the charity is an integral part of the brand proposition. These usually have a long term duration and will add value to the product by drawing on the consumer's affinity with the charity. The most popular use of this technique is the charity affinity credit card. These cards act as an ordinary credit card, but every time they are used, a small percentage of the transaction is donated to the benefiting charity.

Employee fund raising (*See also separate section on 'Employee fund raising'*)

An exercise in which the staff of a company join together to raise funds for a charity or cause. It encompasses any form of fund raising involving employees, their families, friends, past employees and company pensioners.

1 Charity of the Year is an employee fund-raising exercise where the employees or the board of directors of a company have chosen to raise funds for a charity over a set period, which could be six months or three years. These initiatives often extend to customers, suppliers and the local community, but they are always employee driven.
2 Charity Adoption is similar to Charity of the Year, but is usually an on-going activity whereby the company organises occasional events for the chosen charity.

   (a) Employee volunteer schemes are usually instigated by large employers whose employees are encouraged to give a few hours each week/month to work on local community projects.

Some employers allow this time to be taken during normal working hours.

(b) Give As You Earn (GAYE) is often an integral part of employee fund raising, but it is an independently tax efficient means for an individual to support charities on an on-going basis. The employer needs to instigate such a scheme by registering with a charity agency to administer the scheme.

Licensing

This allows the charity's name or logo to be branded on a company's product or service, in return for a royalty. There are also further technical applications for exploiting Information and Technology rights.

Corporate hospitality

This usually involves selling tickets or ticket packages to companies so that they can entertain their staff, clients or potential clients at an event run by the charity.

Secondment

Where company employees are assigned to a charity for a given amount of time, to undertake a specific project. Therefore, the charity receives the benefit of the employee's expertise while the company continues to pay the employee's salary, (although the charity will usually cover expenses incurred while working on the project).

—— Company sponsorship ——

Sponsorship is an established part of the marketing mix, an option regularly used by companies to fulfil specific or general marketing objectives. Organisations can gain company sponsorship for their activities provided they recognise from the outset that they are entering into a commercial agreement that will benefit the company as well as themselves. This is, of course, a trading activity, i.e. you are selling benefits for which the company is paying market value. Therefore, be aware that VAT will apply. You will need to think commercially in terms of distilling a range of benefits, preferably measurable, from whatever you want to get sponsorship for. Not-for-profit is now the fourth option a company has when considering sponsorship, after sport, arts and media. It is also the option with the least credibility in the market place, and charities seeking this type of support should make every effort to enhance the image and credibility of not-for-profit sponsorship opportunities.

The benefits and returns a company will look for from sponsorship may be:

- corporate image enhancement
- product awareness
- hospitality opportunities
- employee loyalty and interest
- improved contact with opinion formers
- part of a product launch initiative
- targeting specific consumers and reaching new markets.

The two key resources you will need to be successful in sponsorship are time and manpower. As a charity you need to agree who is going to be responsible for this and how much of their time will be dedicated to it. If you are a voluntary group or a solo fund raiser, you may decide to recruit someone specifically to look at this area. This fund-raising technique tends to appeal to retired business people who know the corporate world and understand how it operates; ex-marketeers are ideal. So, if you need a new recruit, why not place an advertisement in the local paper, asking for a volunteer to *help you build relationships with the commercial sector*. Once you have established who will be dealing with this area, you should get them to review *any* commercial contact you have had to date, who they were, how they contacted you, or vice versa, and what they did for you. Even a local company who gave a small donation can be important in an audit of commercial contacts to date.

The next step is to review exactly what you believe your charity has that will be suitable for development into commercial sponsorship opportunities. You will need to look at every aspect of the charity and some of the areas you identify may include:

- events
- campaigns
- direct mail
- annual reports
- annual charity weeks
- information leaflets
- transport

● awareness advertising.

It is possible to develop benefit packages from all of the above, depending on your charity's approach and level of activity. These areas should then be put into some order of priority.

After establishing the portfolio of opportunities and the resources to market them, you should review the ethics of working with companies. Considerable time is spent at every training course on corporate fund raising debating this area, but each individual charity must agree its own view of companies alignments for the charity name and objectives. This discussion should take place at the highest level and the agreed guidelines should be clearly set out. Do not compile a black list of companies, but do define trading activity areas that would not be acceptable, e.g. tobacco companies and health charities are obviously incompatible.

The sponsorship proposal

Everyone wants the magic formula for the best possible sponsorship proposal; there isn't one. Different people in different organisations require individual approaches. In my experience, the two keys to success are:

1 Believe in the package you are selling
2 Put yourself in the place of the person you are targeting.

Your project

Look carefully at the project you intend to offer to the sponsor; note exactly what the company will be getting as part of the sponsorship package. For instance, if you are trying to obtain sponsorship for an event, consider:

● Can the company name and logo go on invitations, posters, leaflets, tickets, score cards, programmes, etc?
● Could an exhibition be mounted at the event?
● What opportunities are available for hospitality?
● Could products be given out as prizes, or are there sampling opportunities?
● What advertising will be taken prior to the event and could the sponsor's name be included in it?
● Can a list of names and addresses be supplied as a mailing list after the event?

- Is there an opportunity for sales promotion?
- Have you got the resources to handle the PR or are you looking to the sponsor to handle this aspect?

Price

The price of a sponsorship package should be based on its *value* and not its cost. Once you have worked out the benefits you are able to offer a sponsor, you need to estimate the commercial value of those benefits. Try to find equivalent benefits available elsewhere commercially, e.g. if you are going to reach 50,000 households, how much would it cost to leaflet drop the same number? If in doubt, seek advice from any contacts you may have in PR, marketing or general business. Experience is a key factor in pricing a package accurately.

Some people leave the price of a package *loose*, even to the extent of not including it in an initial approach. If you expect someone to give full consideration to your proposal, they should have all the facts available, including the price.

> NB: In the United Kingdom sponsorship is subject to VAT and you should outline clearly the two figures in your proposal; how much you want and how much the company will have to pay, including VAT.

Finding possible buyers

Once you have written your proposal, you will need to list suitable target companies. This is a buyer's market with several proposals chasing each buyer. Begin your campaign with a brainstorming session; centre your principal object on the paper and think of all the connected subjects. Develop them into lists of connected companies.

(Appendix V lists some of the reference books that will give addresses and basic information on target companies.)

Market information on company public affairs, advertising, product launches, sales promotions and general expansion will provide some guidelines for making the right approach to the right company. This information will be found by regularly reviewing the following journals:

- *PR Week*
- *Campaign*
- *Marketing*
- *National and regional newspapers*
- *Financial Times*
- *The Economist*
- *Business Age*
- *Corporate Citizen Magazine (Directory of Social Change)*

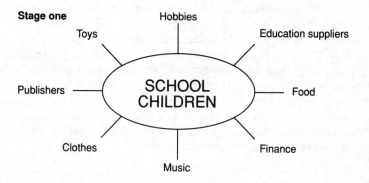

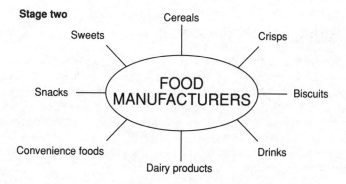

Figure 7 An example of how you might brainstorm sponsorship for a schools pack

Making your approach

There is no set formula as to how you approach a company; different methods work for different people. When starting out, it is better to explore a variety of approaches, carefully assessing the success, time and comfort factors for each approach. The chart, *Reaching companies*, illustrates the many ways you can achieve an approach. My preference is always to try to speak to the relevant person on the telephone first, or at least to speak to the account manager in a company's marketing or PR agency, before approaching the company. Cold letters are probably the least successful method and most companies are inundated with this type of approach, so originality and imagination are essential for gaining company sponsorship. As sponsorship is a business proposition, you should be targeting the commercial side of the company, usually through the marketing department. In many of the larger companies this can be quite a large department, so you will not necessarily be writing to the marketing director. You may find that brand managers are more interested and responsive to your proposals. Company agencies are still greatly under-used by charities when approaching companies. Remember, many of these agencies are employed to come up with good ideas and new solutions to business problems.

Although you will approach a company with one specific sponsorship, keep an open mind and a flexible attitude, since you may have the opportunity to introduce some of your other sponsorship packages. Once you have managed to secure a meeting, you will need to read the situation in order to ensure a sale.

Managing your relationship

Once you have sold the sponsorship, you must ensure that you have a contract with your sponsor. *This is mandatory under the terms of the new Charities Act.* The contract must state who is entering into the agreement; exactly what it entails from both sides; copyright on the logo, etc; what the financial agreement is, including payment date, renewal options and evaluation. This may sound formidable, but it is absolutely necessary to protect your organisation and the company; it also ensures full accountability on the transaction.

While it is possible to outline a contract yourself, it is advisable to seek legal advice, particularly on your initial contracts, until a standard pattern emerges. In view of the expense of legal advice, you may be tempted to rely on the sponsoring company's lawyer to draw up a contract, but you should still seek independent advice to ensure that the contract is a true reflection of your agreement and does not leave you liable to any unforeseen expenses.

Following the exchange of contracts, your project will commence. At this point, you should set up regular liaison meetings with your sponsor to keep them up-dated on progress. This will also allow for any necessary approval of design, event format, etc. Remember, you have sold a commercial opportunity which you now have to deliver. This should be done with the highest possible level of service to ensure that your sponsor is satisfied and will wish to come back for more.

Even when a sponsorship is finished, maintain passive contact with your sponsor, since you never know when you might need their support or advice again.

Sales promotions

This is an advanced fund-raising technique involving a detailed knowledge of the law and trading by charities. Larger charities are pro-active in targeting this area, employing specialist marketeers or agencies. Even then, most large promotional opportunities tend to occur when a company has been pro-active in identifying a charity partner. Awareness of the work of your charity and its name is important, but it can be on a local or regional scale, as well as at national level.

A promotion is any communication that tries to persuade or encourage people to purchase something. Companies use promotions to target the general public, a particular consumer group, trade audiences, franchises, dealers, or their own staff. The options for a company may encompass free offers, self liquidators (an item offered to a customer at basic cost), competitions, price offers or proof of purchase for an offer. Charities are a recognised option within this, with a solid commercial track record to prove their value. Charity in the sales promotion context can:

- create awareness and interest
- increase loyalty

- achieve extra displays for products
- encourage repeat purchases
- increase trial
- deflect attention from price.

Despite all these benefits, the charity and the company must recognise the self-interest of the consumer when designing the promotion.

Being pro-active

If you are ready to extend your fund raising into this technique, the following is a simple starting exercise:

1 Review companies and markets with a natural link or affinity with your cause.
2 Research any trends, innovations and general activities.
3 Brainstorm suitable ideas to meet marketing objectives for a specific product or company.
4 Attempt to reach an agreement, confirm commitments and move to drawing up a contract since this is a legal necessity. The Charities Act prohibits a commercial participator from soliciting money for a charitable institution unless they are acting under an agreement that satisfies the requirements of the Charities Act. If a promotion states that a charitable contribution will be made as a result of the promotion, it *must* specifically identify the institution and the method by which the amount will be determined. Charities and companies must make all books and paperwork in connection with the promotion available on request.

In addition to approaching companies with ideas for promotions, you may be able to encourage them to give you a specific brief to fulfil; in other words, they will use you like a sales promotions agency. Being pro-active in this area requires considerable resources, skills and patience. For small charities, a more effective use of time in developing sales promotion may be to adapt large, successful national promotions to a local model. For example, you may be able to persuade a local car dealership to run a promotion whereby they will donate £5 for everyone who test drives a new car in August. This could be promoted to your existing supporters, advertised in the local paper and promoted at the dealership itself.

Being reactive

With any form of market awareness of your charity, either national or regional, you should be prepared for any calls you may receive from companies or agencies showing an interest in using your cause in their promotional activities. Remember, the main reason for a call in connection with promotions will be for commercial gain by the company, interest in your cause comes next.

REACTIVE CHECK LIST

1 Establish exactly what the proposal is.
2 Who are you talking to, a company or agency? If it is an agency, are they retained by the company or pitching for business?
3 With agencies, try to establish the name of the client, but this may be confidential.
4 What type of promotion is it? Who are the target audience? What is the timing and what is the budget?
5 What exactly does the client or agency expect from the charity?
6 Respond promptly to any requests for further details on the charity or proposals and ensure that you confirm your understanding of the initial call.
7 If you are dealing through an agency, ensure that you meet the client as soon as it is appropriate.
8 Move on to an agreement (as in point 4 of Being pro-active above).

If a company does approach you, remember they identified your cause as suitable for their promotion, so ensure that you negotiate an advantageous package that your supporters will like. Your cause, your image and your logo have value, so do not allow companies or agencies to bully you into unbalanced, unprofitable or unsuitable promotions.

For technical information on sales promotions, training details or codes of practice, contact the Institute of Sales Promotions (See Appendix III).

Figure 8 Degrees of charity involvement in promotions

——— Employee fund raising ———

This can involve three or three hundred people within a company join-ing together to raise funds for an organisation. It is not a new tech-nique, but because more charities are now targeting this area, you will need to consider carefully to ensure that your cause benefits from these activities. Major employee fund-raising initiatives grew in the late seventies as a result of:

- increasing pressure on corporate support
- greater focus on employee health
- its impact on motivation and attendance
- improved on-site company facilities
- increased leisure time and reduction in working hours.

As the number of successful case studies has grown, more companies have reviewed the area, and as the technique has grown in popularity it has become the main area for soliciting major funding from a company.

Some of the benefits to a company can include:

- increased funds from the company to a charity, but it should not be viewed as a substitute for other corporate funding
- improved staff morale, internal relationships, team spirit
- external publicity, especially in local and specialist media
- a more involved form of fund raising
- an opportunity for management development.

A successful employee fund raising scheme needs:

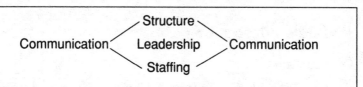

Communication   Structure / Leadership \ Communication   Staffing

Preferably at all levels and objectives led from the top, motivation led from the bottom.

Beginning to think about companies

If you are a well known local or national organisation, it is possible that a company will approach you with an enquiry about organising an employee fund raising initiative, but to secure this type of initiative, it is better to be pro-active and identify targets. The way to identify possible target companies is to:

- identify and research companies who run employee choice systems, where employees vote each year for a charity to receive company support;
- take note of companies who publicise employee fund-raising initiatives through the media and then apply to be their next charity;
- research companies who offer £ for £ matching or other incentives for employee fund-raising initiatives. Some companies even offer time off for employees to undertake volunteering in the community and this can be a major incentive;
- look for companies with active sports and social clubs; particularly companies who provide facilities for these activities;
- identify companies with a link, common interest or affinity to your cause, e.g. pharmaceutical companies and cancer research;
- note those companies trying to reinforce or build their identity through advertising;
- approach companies who are planning anniversary celebrations for

employee fund raising, but you must think ahead and identify companies who will celebrate an anniversary in one or two years time so that they can consider your proposals as part of their celebrations;

- suggest the usefulness of employee fund raising to companies with a new corporate image or identity;
- review former company contacts and discuss employee fund raising to renew the contact.

Possible approaches

Introductions

From your network of contacts try to identify people who may be able to introduce you to a company. Even companies you are already working with may help to introduce you to other companies in their sector.

Piggyback

I constantly emphasise the importance of relationships and, once you have established a link with a company, you should consider how you can introduce employee fund raising as an additional aspect of your relationship with the company. If you receive a donation from their charitable budget, they may not have thought about using this gift to challenge their employees to match it. This type of approach depends on an already established rapport with the company.

Targeting

Although this can be a *cold* approach, you should be aiming to find a reason or a *hook* for your approach. Rather than a blanket mailing, this should only go to selected companies where your research indicates a strong link.

Mole syndrome

Try to find people on the inside. Every charity has enthusiastic volunteers who work in local companies. Sell them the idea of employee fund raising and encourage them to set up initiatives within their own companies. This may initially reach only one department within the company, but it may attract corporate attention and lead to larger initiatives. Most offices have a *mole* who will organise outings, parties and charitable activities. Finding that person and motivating them to support your cause is the key success in this area.

Developing your proposition

Employee fund-raising initiatives can vary in scale and it is often a matter of using or adapting the many other fund-raising techniques outlined in this book. However, with some of the larger opportunities you will need to be prepared to present your case: the reason why a group of employees or a company should choose your cause. This will either be a written presentation or you may be invited to present to a group of employees, a manager or even the board of a company. A typical proposal should cover three elements.

The cause

This should be succinctly presented in a way that is relevant to the company. Say why it is going to motivate people to support the cause.

The mechanics

Capture the imagination of the company and demonstrate that you have thought through the whole process of employee fund raising. Prepare simple ideas such as inter-departmental challenges in unconventional sports; list events that people could enter and fund-raising ideas with suggestion sheets for employees. Give people a chance to have fun. Make sure that your fund-raising mechanics have wide-ranging appeal, using brain as well as brawn.

Larger employee fund-raising initiatives tend to need something different to attract interest and participation, but do not forget to support these ideas with conventional methods of charitable support such as payroll giving and covenants.

Motivation

If the cause and the mechanics are right, this element should follow naturally. Never forget, however, the importance of communication at every stage of your initiative. Publicise widely and ensure that everyone is kept abreast of progress and the results. Some companies choose to offer £ for £ matching with employee fund raising and this is a major motivator. Sometimes suppliers are persuaded to offer prizes and other incentives, but even without these, simple trophies can motivate and drive people to achieve their target.

These are the main areas to be covered in any proposal or presentation, but you should always remember that an employer's requirements from you can range from expecting nothing to expecting everything. If this is a new area for you, it may be even newer for the company and they will require your support, expertise and ideas.

Summary

Encourage this opportunity for fund raising wherever possible, whether it involves two employees or the whole company. Do, however, consider your resources and the commitment necessary if you are going to attempt to secure larger opportunities. Be realistic when discussing opportunities with companies and do not promise what you cannot deliver. Some major schemes may need seed money to start the initiatives and, if you cannot afford this, ask the company to pay – they can only refuse. Some of the smaller initiatives in this field can offer the best models and frameworks for development, so monitor all relevant activies.

———————— Payroll giving ————————

Until 1987 the only way for a company employee to make a tax efficient gift to a charity was by a legally binding commitment from the individual for four years or more. This has now changed with the introduction of payroll giving. This scheme enables any person on a payroll to give to charity from their pre-tax pay. Payroll giving is an entirely voluntary activity for both the employee and employer, open to all employees from all sectors. The employee simply chooses to participate in the scheme, selecting the level of donation (up to £900 per annum), and this is deducted from their pay and passed on to an agency for distribution to the charities nominated by the employee.

The whole process starts when an employer decides to offer this scheme to employees. It must be registered with a charity agency, approved by the Inland Revenue, such as the Charities Aid Foundation (CAF) where the scheme is known as Give as You Earn (GAYE), or the Charities Trust whose scheme is known as Work Aid. These and smaller agencies promote payroll giving and support charities who are active in this area. But their primary function is to receive money donated by employees

HOW PAYROLL GIVING WORKS

Employer agrees to participate

↓

Chooses and registers with agency charity

↓

Scheme promotion

↓

Employee chooses charity and amount of donation

↓

Form returned to payroll office

↓

Appropriate deduction made to salary and forwarded to agency charity

↓

Agency donation to *bona fide* charity

and to ensure that it is passed on to the chosen *registered* charities. The agency is entitled to deduct up to 5 per cent of the donation to cover their administration costs. Charities are totally responsible for making themselves and their needs known to the employees.

Once registered, an employer will make forms available to employees so that they may specify the amount they wish to donate (gross) and the charity or charities they wish to receive the donation. The form is returned to the employer to enable them to make the appropriate deductions from the employee's salary, and combine all the donations throughout the company to be forwarded at a specified time to the agency in one payment. Employees do not have to declare their choice of charities to anyone other than the agency, and the forms are designed to ensure this confidentiality. The charity will receive its donation gross and does not have to reclaim tax, unlike in the covenant procedure.

Payroll giving is still a very new method of giving to charity, with considerable potential for development. Although the scheme has been operating for several years, it is used by less than 10 per cent of UK donors, and more work needs to be done by charities to promote the scheme. Charities must ensure that all employers are registered to operate the scheme and then promote its ease and effectiveness to the employees. Charities should regard this as a means of building a regular income, often with new donors, and probably one of the easiest ways of capitalising on tax efficient giving.

Promoting payroll giving

Successful payroll promotion is usually the result of a two-pronged approach from the employer and charity. The charity must create a specific interest in their cause and *close* the interest by signing employees up to the scheme. It relies on a pro-active approach; you may gain donors simply by being there, but to build up a reasonable income and a donor base, you need to decide on a promotional strategy, tailored to the cause and your resources.

First, ascertain whether the company is already registered with an agency charity. If not, persuade the company to register and help them to do this. Approach a director level in small companies and through the personnel department in medium and large companies. Then contact one of the agency charities to support you and to carry out the registration. When the company is registered, identify the best means of approaching employees to promote your cause. The personnel or finance department should be able to help you open up communication channels to the employees. Most employers are aware of the scheme, but, outside the major companies, pressure to take part usually comes from employees. Companies see this as a service to staff that promotes the *caring company* image. The most common objection to the scheme is that it creates an extra burden of administration, but the agency charities can soon demonstrate that this is not actually the case. Some tips for promoting payroll giving are listed below:

One to one promotion

Face to face meetings are the most effective means of creating an understanding of a charity's work and its needs. Companies sometimes allow shop floor meetings, in the canteen or at specially created sessions, but you will need to convince managers that this type of opportunity is a worthwhile investment of time. Trade unions can also help by allowing access to union meetings. Where a company is divided into departments, it may be possible to persuade department heads to allow you a ten minute slot at team meetings. Staff consultative committees are also good sources of direct access to employees.

You should seek to identify and gain the support of two or three employees who would be willing to promote payroll giving to their colleagues. It is well worth training such people in the method of operating the scheme and discussing how they can best promote it within the company. People will support you through payroll giving because:

- the cause appeals to them
- they have been asked for support
- it is tax efficient
- they are subject to peer group pressure.

Promotional material

It is worth producing a simple leaflet outlining the key selling points and reasons why a donor should choose your charity. Make this as specific as possible, showing how important small, regular donations can be; show how valuable a donation of £50 a month would be to the charity.

Use these leaflets in your one to one promotions, but also ask employers to make them available in rest areas, canteens, personnel departments, finance departments, etc. Local authorities have allowed me to attach to pay slips and this is an effective way of ensuring that every employee receives a copy.

Posters (A4 and A3 size) are also a useful way of reminding employees about the scheme. Do not be tempted to produce larger posters since it is unlikely that you will be allocated sufficient space to display them. Keep your poster simple and use it with a company where it is acceptable for staff notice boards, canteens, reception areas and lifts.

Some charities use items such as pens, T-shirts and logo bugs, but these are an expensive method of promotion, unless you are invited to participate in a charity fair where employees are encouraged to shop around and select their charity. They can be used as a means of thanking donors, but it is important not to create an impression of extravagance.

Combine forces

Charity consortia can be very effective in gaining access to a company.

Employers like the unbiased approach of allowing a group of non-competitive charities to have access to their employees. The main types of consortia are:

- a broad spectrum of causes, e.g. animals, children's, medical research, homelessness, etc;
- a complementary group of charities in the same field, e.g. a group of children's charities.

This approach works just as well at national and local levels, so consider combining forces with other local causes in either of these categories and you will save costs on promotional materials and effort. To comply with the Charities Act, you should ensure that you can and do incorporate a statement such as; *all of which are registered charities*.

Agency support

There are now some agencies who specialise in supporting charities with payroll giving. Their staff will approach companies, set up appointments, make presentations and, in effect, do the work for you. If they actually solicit the donation or the pledge of the donation, they are deemed to be Professional Fund Raisers under Part II of the Charities Act. They will probably charge a basic fee plus an additional payment for each employee who signs up. This can make the process initially expensive, particularly when you consider how much of the first annual donation is available for your cause. In the long term, however, the figures may be more appealing. Consider these opportunities carefully, as you are entrusting the good name of your charity to a third party.

—— Company grant applications ——

Companies annually set aside a proportion of their profits to allocate to charities who meet agreed criteria. The charity committee or company secretary administer the donation of such funds in a manner similar to a grant making trust. *The Guide to Company Giving*, Directory of Social Change, lists the objectives of company giving, as will an annual report, and a telephone call will often elicit information about company policy towards donations. Again, this is a competitive area and some companies are beginning to look for commercial benefits for their charitable donations. True corporate philanthropy is now static, if not in decline.

The skills and techniques used to apply for trust donations also apply to company approaches, particularly the outline of the application; (*see section on 'Trusts and foundations' in Chapter 11*).

The charity fund of many companies is being used increasingly to promote employee fund raising. Employees are offered matching donations to the charity of their choice to a defined upper limit. If you are approached by individuals who want to donate funds raised by a sponsored activity, always ask whether they have approached their company for matching funding. If you already know that a company offers matching funding, ask local groups to contact the employees of the company to encourage them to raise funds; (*see section on 'Employee fund raising'*).

PHONE CALL To establish the right person to contact	**LETTER/PROPOSAL** Saying you will ring them	**PHONE CALL** To discuss proposal and establish interest	**MEETING** Hopefully!
PHONE CALL To book a general meeting to discuss the charity and opportunities	**MEETING** To have a general discussion/presentation and talk about possibilities	**LETTER/PROPOSAL** Having developed and tailored one of the possibilities	**PHONE CALL** To establish interest and develop further ideas and the proposal
INTRODUCTION Via a Trustee, Director, contact or friend of the charity	**MEETING** Presentation on the charity and a shopping list of ideas; commercial and non-commercial	**LETTER/PROPOSAL** Having developed and tailored something off the shopping list	**PHONE CALL** To establish interest and develop further ideas and the proposal
PHONE CALL To discuss your specific sponsorship package in broad outline and to establish interest	**LETTER/PROPOSAL** Confirming details of your discussion	**PHONE CALL** To establish interest and to arrange a meeting	**MEETING** Hopefully!
PHONE CALL To the company's agency to discuss suitability/ possibility or the idea of working with the company	**LETTER/PROPOSAL** To the agency or direct to the company for consideration	**PRESENTATION** To the agency describing the charity and its potential to work with their client	**PHONE CALL/MEETING** Call to the company or agency to establish interest or A further meeting with the agency and their clients

10

DIRECT MARKETING

This chapter describes many different techniques, but their common aim is to communicate your organisation's proposition directly to an existing or a potential donor, thereby exploiting a direct relationship. Such contact builds up a relationship and enables you to achieve a better understanding of your donor. By keeping records and analysing information you can enhance the productivity of your relationship.

Direct marketing is about the four Rs:

- *the* Right person
- *with the* Right message
- *at the* Right time
- *using the* Right approach.

Direct marketing is distinct from conventional advertising in that it is infinitely targetable, has a direct response, is measurable and enables you to build a database (or for small charities a detailed record system). Charities use direct marketing in three key areas:

- fund raising
- awareness
- campaigning.

The media and methods involved are principally:

- press
- direct mail
- radio
- television
- telephone
- inserts

- household distribution/door drop
- electronic.

Direct marketing uses these media within the commercial and charity worlds, but charities are trying to sell a concept, not a product, and to generate empathy. It is worth remembering the four key human traits that respond to charity direct marketing:

- compassion
- guilt
- fear
- self esteem.

To provoke a response to your proposition, remember AIDCA:

- **Attention:** without it you won't succeed
- **Interest:** why should they be interested?
- **Desire:** remember the human traits
- **Conviction:** if you don't believe it, neither will the donor
- **Action:** make it clear and easy.

Press advertising

Pick up any of the quality press and you will see a variety of direct response advertisements being used by charities to recruit donors. They usually occupy key positions in carefully selected newspapers. Every aspect of the advertisement has been considered and tested, or at least it should have been, in order to achieve the greatest chance of success. While you will see other forms of charity advertising regularly in papers, you can always distinguish direct response advertisements by applying the AIDCA formula. Press advertising can cover any publication that will sell or donate advertising space to enable you to put across your message. So, before you dismiss this area as one only suitable for large charities, remember that you should be able to tailor your resources and buying power and find a suitable publication in which to test this technique. I will discuss the possibility of free space later.

Charities who use press advertising regularly, generally agree that it is an extremely effective way of reaching potential donors, but it is not a means of raising short-term funds, except in emergency or disaster appeals. Breaking even or making a small profit is the accepted norm and you are unlikely to make a large surplus out of this technique. The objective is to secure donors who will have a lifetime of value and you will have a pay back in the medium to long term. (Remember the donor pyramid — figure 3).

Advertising is a technical area that requires a wide range of skills and experience, but even a small local charity can acquire the basic understanding of the key elements needed to place an advertisement without incurring the cost of a specialist agency. Much can be learned simply by looking at a variety of publications to see the style of advertising undertaken by other charities, particularly the large nationals who probably do have an agency supporting this type of work. Where are they placing their advertisement? Next to the crossword, on the front page, bottom right hand side of the page? Do they use an attention grabbing headline or a dramatic picture and strong and tightly edited copy? What format does the response coupon take; or is the call to action a telephone response? Are they consistently using the same approach?

As with all fund raising, start from the donor. What is the profile of the potential donor, what do they read? You do not have to be particularly technical about this; larger publications produce a media pack giving a profile of their readers. If you are advertising in the local parish magazine, you will need a profile of the local parishioners and active church members. Your selection of media is made easier by connecting publications to the type of reader and then potential donor. Next ask yourself what message will grab the attention of a reader? Charities use a variety of styles in this type of advertising and are constantly seeking to be innovative. Some of the styles you may see are:

- *dramatic picture* – not necessarily a negative image, but one that will attract the reader's attention and communicate a message;
- *bold headline* – something that people cannot fail to notice, or a statement to which your potential donor will relate;
- *something different* – a combination of words, pictures, illustration and layout that stands out from the page;
- *familiarity* – a typical theme in this type of advertising may be a celebrity or local figurehead who is recognised by people. Again, make sure they relate to your particular donor;
- *shopping lists* – I am sure you will have seen the RNLI style of advertisement with the picture of a lifeboatman standing in his

full kit, with arrows showing the cost of each element;

- *handwritten* – again, used to make the advertisement stand out and attract attention. Sometimes used to convey a deserving, amateur feel to the advertisement. Using the print style of an old typewriter also falls into this category;
- *spot colour* – depending on the publication, this can be expensive, but eye catching;
- *not a charity* – a challenge or puzzle for the reader to draw them into the advertisement and to convey your message;
- *innovation* – look at everyone else's advertisements and then be different.

Having considered publication, position and content, you should think of response mechanism and review. The most tried and tested response mechanism is the coupon, asking for name, address, post-code, amount of donation (this may be specific to the message in the advertisement), and the method of payment. Payment can be by cheque, postal order or credit card (if you are set up for this method of payment). Your return address can also be important in that donors prefer to write to an individual they feel they can trust, rather than just a Post Office box number. If possible, link the person receiving return donations to the content or story of the advertisement. You may also wish to consider a Freepost address, but this will add to your costs. A telephone number can be used as a response mechanism but you must ensure that you are equipped to handle a higher than anticipated level of response, or otherwise use an agency to deal with this. The telephone can also limit the times when a donor can give, can you really offer a 24 hour service, or will they have access to a telephone when they wish to respond? When thinking of using the telephone for this, talk to British Telecom, Mercury or other service providers about Freephone or local charge numbers, they may increase your response rate and are well worth investigating.

Never undertake any advertising without building in a review mecha-nism. Quite simply, if you are placing an advertisement, give it a unique code that will help you to identify the source of any response. This way you can assess the real costs of advertising and what has worked well.

I have focused on a standard type of advertisement, usually 20cm × 2 columns, but all of the principles outlined in this section can work just as well for much smaller advertisements. In fact, many charities now take standard small advertisements in newspapers, or incorporate themselves within unusual sections of a paper, e.g. the personal or births and deaths column.

All newspapers have a rate card showing the cost of the different sizes of advertising space. This is a fictional guideline that no one ever pays, and you should use all of your negotiating skills to ensure the largest possible discount on any space you buy. Advertising is a competitive area and it is time-sensitive in terms of selling space before print deadlines. Therefore it is not impossible to secure free advertising space. You will need to have an advertisement and miscellaneous coupon codes in a form ready for publication and, following a request to the publication, if they are sympathetic they will keep your advertisement on hold ready for any unsold space they may have. Of course, you do not have much control over the timing, but the paper may give you an indication of how long you may have to wait.

All advertising must comply with the Code of Advertising Practice, administered by the Advertising Standards Authority and must contain all registered charity information.

Think about your reaction to advertisements and how you read different publications, then apply this to developing your advertising strategy. Finally, remember that the direct response does not have to be a way of immediate fund raising, it may be a way of encouraging people towards making covenants, making a will, regular giving or, as some charities are testing, participation in an event.

——— Sponsored advertising ———

The following guidelines are designed for fund raisers on a local level, to help them obtain sponsored advertising space in their local newspapers.

Getting started

1 Obtain copies of the newspaper you propose to approach. It is useful to be able to say that you read the paper when talking to them or to potential sponsors of this exercise.
2 Telephone the display advertising manager of the paper you have

selected and find out:

(*a*) Circulation and readership figures.

(*b*) Whether the paper is one of a larger series.

(*c*) If the charity were to buy a full page of advertising, what sort of discount could they expect? You will probably need the registered charity number to hand before you will be given this information.

(*d*) If they would be willing to approach their regular advertisers to sponsor the page in whole or in part for you. This may be an appropriate way for the local paper to support your charity or even a useful training aid for their telesales department. Either way, from past experience, local papers are on the whole willing to help in this way. If they agree to take on the whole exercise, it will naturally be to suit their time-frame, but it is worth agreeing the number of sponsors you require to meet the costs and the division of total costs (e.g. a space costing £1,000 may require 10 sponsors at £100 or 20 sponsors at £50).

(*e*) If they will not take on the whole exercise, they may agree that, if you obtain 50 per cent of the total costs needed, then their telesales department will take on the other 50 per cent.

(*f*) Be aware of the requirements of Part II of the Charities Act.

or

(*g*) If they would be willing to supply you with a list of their regular advertisers (their concern her would be that you would treat such a list in the strictest confidence and promise not to mention such a list in any approaches to advertisers).

or

(*h*) Failing any of the above, if they would be willing to mail you copies of all the papers in their series so that you can make up your own lists of large space advertisers.

With luck, the paper will handle all the sponsorship approaches for you, in which case all you will have to do is telephone the paper and they will do the rest. If not, then it will probably involve a couple of days telephone work to raise the necessary money.

Types of regional newspaper

These fall into two categories:

1 Bought papers: paid for by the public, often they cover large areas,

e.g. a county. These papers are generally expensive to advertise in.

2   Free sheets: free distribution to the public, but usually covering a smaller area, e.g. a town. High density distribution and cheaper advertising rates. Charity discounts usually very good.

The advertisement itself

The content will obviously be linked to your particular need, appeal or campaign; here are some of the areas it could cover:

1   An awareness campaign: giving the public general information about your charity and its objectives. This obviously serves to heighten people's awareness so that, if they are approached locally or nationally for support of some kind, they would already have some knowledge of the charity. Most of the large national charities undertake national awareness campaigns at some time, usually linked to an anniversary.

2   Specific appeal: could be for a local hospice, cathedral restoration, etc. This type of sponsored advertisement has to be carefully targeted to link a local project with a relevant local paper, as papers will avoid blatant appeals for cash unless they are of prime interest to their readers.

3   An event: the scope in this area is vast, ranging from a local marathon to a charity shop opening. The key being the interest or novelty factor.

The format

There are several different formats for this type of communication, and the paper you are working with will have experience of what they have used in the past. You need to think which of these would be most appropriate for your needs, as the wrong format can create the wrong image.

Here are some possible different formats:

1   The majority of the page is occupied with your advertisement and a list of sponsors is at the bottom of the page, just their names and not their logos. This is by far the best format as it is clear cut and has maximum impact.

2   The charity advertisement appears in the middle of the page and

has a border of small advertisements or acknowledgements around it. This can look reasonably presentable, but only consider this format if the paper is handling the whole exercise, otherwise you will find yourself involved in trying to sort out copy, fit in logos, good luck messages, etc. If the border is too wide, it can also detract from your message/advertisement.

3   The charity shares a page with its sponsors. Usually the top half is given to the charity for its advertisement and the bottom is divided into boxes for use of the sponsors paying for the page. This is a very unattractive option and looks extremely commercial.

In addition to the advertisement, a lot of newspapers will offer you the added bonus of editorial. Even if this is not offered, it is worth asking for. Therefore, you should prepare in advance the sort of editorial you would like to see appear near to your advertisement.

The sponsorship approach

If you are having to handle all or part of the sponsorship approaches yourself, you should by now have a list of all the local companies who advertise in the paper in which you are trying to advertise. Time to get on the telephone.

Bearing in mind that you are contacting small businesses, remember they will have little experience of the sort of approach that you are about to make and very little time to listen to it. Therefore it is essential that you have planned and thought through your telephone approach before ringing.

1   Ask for the managing director, partner, manager, advertising manager, or whatever position would be appropriate considering the type of company your are approaching.

2   Once you have reached your target person, explain what your charity is trying to achieve in the local area and why it needs to support this activity with newspaper advertising.

3   Your target person will probably ask how much you want, negotiate carefully. The starting point obviously comes from research and thinking through the company beforehand, e.g. local butchers – £50; local car dealer – £200, etc.

4   Make sure they realise they will only get a list mention in a Sponsored by ... format at the bottom of your advertisement. As long as you have a clear picture in your mind of the format for

which you are aiming, by this stage a company will not disagree with you.

5 Even if the company has agreed to sponsor part of your advertising, they will probably ask for a letter confirming all the above details on your official headed paper before parting with their sponsorship money. So, in preparing for this exercise, you should think of the sort of format you want for these letters, bearing in mind that this element gives credibility to your approach.

6 You should ask for a cheque at this stage, made payable to your charity for the agreed amount, and inform the sponsor that you will, of course, be sending them an invoice.

7 It is important to set up a logical accounting process for this exercise, to ensure that you know exactly where you stand and so that you can inform the newspaper when you have the full cost of your advertisement.

8 Even if the newspaper has agreed to handle all or part of the sponsorship through its telesales team, it is important that cheques from sponsors are made payable to your charity and that these all come to you for processing and thank you letters. You would then require the paper to invoice your charity for the agreed discounted rate.

Direct mail

This is exactly what it says: getting a piece of mail to a named individual. As the fastest growing advertising medium, accounting for over 25 per cent of all advertising expenditure, you would expect it to be a complex and sophisticated area. It is, but this does not exclude it from any organisation that is willing to take the time to grasp the basics and have a go. The following guidelines are only intended as the basics, and as you begin to develop this area and gain some success, you will need to expand your knowledge through more detailed books on the subject. Most charities are active in the direct mail area:

- they can accurately target potential donors
- it is personal and, therefore, very powerful; people give to people and people like getting letters from friends;
- it is very flexible;
- once established, it is predictable and cost effective;
- it allows you to test ideas/propositions and to be creative.

You may be thinking how much you dislike direct mail. It is on the increase, but charities would not continue to invest in a technique that is not making a handsome profit and, therefore, raising vital funds.

The uses of direct mail in fund raising are primarily:

- appeals
- membership
- catalogues/trading
- corporate sponsorship
- legacy marketing
- building relationships.

As always, you should start with the donor and ask yourself whether you are intending to use direct mail to build better relationships with existing donors and, therefore, secure larger or more frequent donations, or are you going to use direct mail to reach new potential donors with your cause. A small organisation will have the advantage of a more personal local approach, which should stand out from some of the more sophisticated mailings being used by larger charities.

From either of these two audiences you will need to establish a list of names and addresses, preferably with postcodes. Naturally, you will have a list of established supporters, but potential ones may have to be bought in from a list broker, other organisations who own lists or a mailing house. If you are going to buy lists, you must have an idea of the profile of your existing donors and, therefore, the type of people to whom your cause will appeal. In describing people, you will find it helpful to familiarise yourself with a demographic profiling system such as NRS Social Grade Definitions (see Appendix II).

Starting from the list of potential targets is important, as the list element of your direct mail is twice as influential as the offer within the letter.

If this is your first venture into direct mail, you should certainly start from your in-house list, which will involve fewer risks and should yield higher returns. If you have not been involved in building the list of donors, try to establish a history of how the list came into being. As you can imagine, a direct mail list is a perishable commodity, and many charities have wasted a great deal of time and money on something that was never really useable in the first place. In developing the history of a list, some of the areas you should consider are:

- Where did the list originate?
- Has it been used before?
  - (a) recency
  - (b) frequently
  - (c) value
- Do you have a profile of people on the list?
  - (a) demographic
  - (b) lifestyle.

Having established a warm list of donors for the foundation of your first venture into direct mail, the next most important element is the offer. Think of the commercial direct mail that you will receive on a daily basis, the offer is often developed around the what is in it for me syndrome. Remember what I said about human emotions aroused by propositions. You have a cause to sell and you need to describe and present either an element of it or the whole thing in a way that will encourage people to respond. Letter writing is another specialist skill, but there is no reason why you cannot develop your style in a way that will encourage people to support your cause. Remember that, behind your offer should be your objective for undertaking the whole exercise, what do you want the donor to do? How do you want them to respond?

The letter

- Think about the reader as you write the letter. Is there sufficient interest and should they read on?
- Does the letter grab their attention the minute they look at it? You only have seconds before it is discarded, unless there is a good reason to persevere.
- If they make a donation, what will the real effect be? Can they change something or make a difference?
- Be sincere in your style. If you do not believe in it and convey passion and enthusiasm, the donor will not.
- Create a sense of urgency.
- Include an easy and understandable call to action.

I am sure you are familiar with the standard layout of a letter, but look at some of the letters you receive in either commercial or charity direct mail. You may notice that:

- they tend to be longer
- they use headlines to attract your attention

- the salutation is usually personalised
- the signature looks genuine
- the bottom of the letter has a PS
- the letter is broken up into easy to read paragraphs
- there is no jargon and the use of words is precise.

The whole package

The letter should be viewed as the heart of your direct mail, but as you will know from mail you receive, this is only one element in most professional direct mail packages. *All elements must include the relevant registered charity information.* Mail packs also include:

Reply device

If this is separate from the letter, it will stand out and make it easier for the donor to respond. As well as a coupon, you should think of a reply envelope, which you may decide to make Freepost or Business Reply, where you will pay the postage. For both of these systems you will need to make prior arrangements with the Post Office. For small mailings you may decide to include a stamped addressed envelope. This can also look more personal. A lot of charities take the view that if a donor is going to take the time to donate, then they will not object to paying the return postage and that donors may see it as a waste of resources to include a pre-paid envelope, even though with Freepost and Business Reply you only pay for the replies received. To gain the best of both worlds, use Freepost and include the option for a donor to put a stamp on, which avoids any charge back to the charity.

Third voice or lift letter

This device is used to reinforce the information in a letter to bring another dimension to it. For example, if Imperial Cancer Research Fund wrote a letter to donors telling them about their breast cancer research programme, they might include a further letter from one of their scientists talking about the financial need within their laboratory to further a particular line of research. Often these letter are reproduced in hand written, memo form, on the particular person's letterhead or in a different size from the other letter. In commercial mailings, this type of letter is usually from a satisfied customer or a summary of benefits for a potential customer who needs convincing.

Leaflets and brochures

The key to these is to make sure that they are relevant and that they enhance the messages in the letter. Too many people include leaflets just because they have them available. As well as giving greater detail of your need and cause in general, leaflets can give you the benefit of being able to include pictures of your work or problem. Remember that a picture can be worth a thousand words. In general beware of including anything that can be perceived as being glossy or expensive.

Involvement devices (gimmicks)

As charity mailings increase, there is more and more pressure on charities to be different and to stand out from the crowd. Remember the importance of grabbing the donor's interest the minute they open the envelope. Some charities have developed some inexpensive additions to mailings that help to involve the donor in the offer:

- an opaque piece of plastic through which the donor looks to experience the defective vision of someone in the developing world afflicted with cataracts;
- a straw that the donor is asked to breath through for a couple of minutes to experience what breathing is like for someone who suffers from asthma;
- a sheet of newspaper described as a blanket to remind donors about the hardships of not having a home or a shelter to go to.

None of these ideas costs more than a few pence, but the results they achieved were quite considerable. Although this type of addition to the mail pack is unlikely to be relevant when you start out in this area, you may have a cause that lends itself to this idea and you may have an inspirational idea that you want to try. I am not aware of local charitable causes using this technique, so it may be worth considering in an attempt to be different.

The envelope

Never to be taken for granted or ignored. Think about your daily mail; you make initial assessments by the envelope and from this you decide which order to open things. The envelope is your shop window, the area that ensures people will enter the shop to look further. Even with the address, an envelope has a lot of blank space that can carry a message or introduction to your offer, but make it relevant. Do not just put your logo on an envelope for effect, this could relegate it to the might open at some stage level. Strong headlines or quotes on the envelope can gain the donor's interest. For effect, a lot of charities choose to produce this message as if written by hand. Make the envelope powerful, but do not try and make it work too hard.

Your objective is to produce a well written package that conveys your message in a way you believe will appeal to your donors; so your package should fit together to convey thought, clarity and continuity. I have incorporated points on the creative aspect throughout my guidelines, but in the early days do not spend too much time on this aspect since it will happen naturally as you develop the various elements of your campaign in general. Remember:

- list = potential donor
- offer
- package and format.

Database

Even if you are starting out your direct mail with only a few hundred donors, you must think about how you store the relevant information on these individuals; how you add to it and update it. The days of doing this manually are gone and computers are within the reach of most people. Many small charities start up with either a donated or second-hand computer. Choosing the right software is vital since it enables you to build a database of donors, which can be developed to include responses and support. Begin to divide your donors (segmentation) by needs and interests and plan your use of them more effectively. Retaining donors is just as important (if not more so) as gaining new ones and a database helps you to use information to build on their loyalty and keep them satisfied. A computer will help you to practise relationship fund raising, provided you plan your database carefully in the first place.

There are many database packages available and numerous specialist companies more than willing to discuss your needs. Before consulting them, write down exactly what you think you require (a specification). This need not be in technical language, but it should say what you want the database for and what you want to retrieve from it. The more work you put into this early part of planning the database, the more benefit you will receive from it. Ask for information packages from half a dozen software companies who specialise in fund-raising needs. You will find advertisements and addresses every month in all the major charity publications: *Professional Fund Raising, Third Sector, Charity Magazine,* etc.

In this area, you must familiarise yourself with the Data Protection Act 1984. The following is an extract from the guidelines published by the Data Protection Registrar:

Data Protection Act 1984

The act requires all those who store personal details on a computer to register their use of that data with the Data Protection Registrar, and to follow certain rules of good information handling practice – detailed below. Failure to register is a criminal offence and charities are in no way exempted from these requirements.

What the act covers

The act only applies to automatically processed information – broadly speaking, information that is processed by a computer. It does not cover information that is held and processed manually – for example, in ordinary paper files.

The Act does not cover all computerised information but only that which relates to living individuals. So, for example, it does not cover information that relates only to a company or organisation and not to an individual.

Because it is dealing with a new subject, the Act uses some unfamiliar words and phrases. It is important to grasp their meaning because they define how the Act works:

Personal data

Information recorded on a computer about living, identifiable individuals. Statements of fact and expressions of opinion about an individual are personal data but an indication of the data user's intentions towards the individual is not.

Data subject

An individual to whom personal data relate.

Data user

People or organisations who control the contents and use of a collection of personal data. A data user will usually be a company, corporation or other organisation but it is possible for an individual to be a data user.

Computer bureaux

People or organisations who process personal data for users or who allow data users to process personal data on their computers.

Data protection principles

Registered data users must comply with the Data Protection Principles in relation to the personal data they hold. The Principles broadly state that personal data shall:

- be obtained and processed fairly and lawfully;
- be held for those purposes and only be disclosed to those people described in the register entry (very important for fund raisers);
- be adequate, relevant and not excessive in relation to the purpose for which they are held;
- be accurate and, where necessary, kept up to date;
- be held no longer than is necessary for the registered purpose;
- be surrounded by proper security.

The Principles also provide for individuals to have access to data held about themselves and, where appropriate, access to have the data corrected or deleted.

To enforce compliance with the Principles, the Registrar can serve three types of notice. They are:

- an enforcement notice, requiring the data user to take specified action to comply with the particular Principle. Failure to comply with the notice would be a criminal offence;
- a de-registration notice, cancelling the whole or part of a data user's register entry. The data user would then be committing an

offence if they continued to treat the personal data subject to the notice as though it was registered;

● a transfer prohibition notice, preventing the data user from transferring personal data overseas if the Registrar is satisfied that the transfer is likely to lead to a Principle being broken. Failure to comply with such a notice is a criminal offence.

A person on whom a notice is served is entitled to appeal against the Registrar's decision to the Data Protection Tribunal.

Costs and expectations of direct mail

Direct mail is a flexible, attractive way of raising funds from your donors and, in the long term, it can be very profitable. However, it is expensive and will only rarely give an immediate return on investment. Compared to the cost ratio of other fund-raising methods, direct mail is the most expensive medium and the more you use it to recruit new donors (cold mailing), the more expensive it becomes in the short to medium term.

As a small organisation or someone just starting out in direct mail, it is difficult to advise how much it is likely to cost you without reviewing the specific objectives and elements of your activity. On the assumption that you are handling a small mailing in house, you will require rental of a mailing list, second class postage and some basic printing; for this you should allow for a unit cost of around 35p (1995 value). Costs will fall as volume increases, but beyond a certain point, depending on your resources, you will need support from outside agencies, thus incurring further charges.

Success in direct mail comes from establishing long term goals and balancing the development of your programme between mailing to existing donors (warm mailings), and cold mailings. Analyse, evaluate and revise every mailing constantly to acquire data and guidelines for the future.

——————— Door drops ———————

Following the principles I have outlined to develop your direct mail pack, there is then another option for distribution of this pack. Simply chose an area and distribute a letter to every household. For a small charity, you may be able to do this using volunteers. For larger distributions there are several companies who can organise it for you. The Royal Mail operates a household delivery service (HDS), where your unaddressed letter would be delivered with normal household mail. The Royal Mail has the country divided into postcode districts and there are demographic profiles of the various districts; so even this method of reaching donors can have a degree of accuracy and predictability. There should be no difference in your mail pack approach for a cold mailing or door drop.

Inserts

This can be viewed as being in the ground between direct mail and press advertising. Develop a leaflet with your offer and request for support and then investigate the possible distribution channels. Inserts fall into two categories:

1 Newspapers, magazines and general publications.
2 Piggy-back mailings where a leaflet about your cause is included in mailings being undertaken by a third party; usually to existing customers of a company.

An insert should be simple yet strong in communicating your message; along the same lines as a press advertisement. There should be no such thing as a standard size for an insert, but most charities, favour A5 paper. Again, reflect on your own perception of inserts in magazines or mailings; do you read them; if so, why? A strong headline or a relevant photograph are good starting points. Remember to include all relevant registered charity information. Some of the most effective inserts are used by membership charities such as RSPB, who have a strong, simple and appealing proposition; or child adoption agencies such as World Vision, who have a fixed price that will make a real difference to a child's life.

With inserts, pay particular attention to the response mechanism. You have more space than in a newspaper advertisement, so use it. The large charities have spent many years perfecting the most effective reply coupon, so build up a selection and design a version to suit your needs.

Inserts are an established advertising opportunity, so most publications and mailings have a price to include your leaflet. These costs are quite reasonable, especially compared to other direct marketing opportunities and, of course, it is always worth asking if the supplier will donate an insert opportunity. Similarly, it is possible to take advantage of last-minute insert opportunities by having pre-printed insert stocks carrying miscellaneous key codes. You will be surprised how few people ask for these opportunities and remember, you do not get what you do not ask for. It is also worth thinking of insert opportunities that are not standard, e.g. an annual mailing to local sports club members, or a local tradesman who invoices his customers by post. Do not be deterred from sending your leaflet out with a bill of some kind, since some of the most successful inserts are included with water rate or gas bills.

Radio

There are two routes available when contemplating the use of radio for reaching donors; paid advertising or free airtime given because your message is newsworthy and of interest to the listeners.

Paid advertising

If you tune into Classic FM for more than two hours, you will hear at least one charity advertisement appealing for support (usually cash donations). These advertisements convey a powerful message in 60 seconds or less; they are usually produced by professionals and elicit the desired response. This is a recent development in the field of charity appeals and there are still many opportunities for newcomers who are prepared to allocate funds to pay for airtime.

I recommend the use of an agency in this area, to co-ordinate the project and to buy the airtime at the right price. This need not be a large agency – there are many who support small local businesses with their radio advertising.

Key considerations
- What messages have worked well in any direct mailing or other

advertising you have undertaken, and will they translate to a
radio advertisement?

● Use a memorable telephone number for the response mechanism.
Ensure that you can handle the response at times when the
advertisement goes out. (An agency may be needed for this.)

● Research the radio station, its profile, listeners, coverage, etc. Is it
the right one for you?

Free radio coverage

In addition to the use of radio for publicity purposes as described in
the section on PR, it can also be used for fund raising in the following
three ways:

1 Existing opportunities

The radio station may have a regular weekly or monthly charity slot
in which local charities are allowed to make an appeal. The BBC (and
some independent stations) has a formal system of applying for one of
these slots and, on receipt of the application, they review the candi-
dates. The successful applicant will receive very specific guidelines on
what can be said and how the response should be managed. Radio 4
broadcasts *The Week's Good Cause*, for which any registered charity
can apply. Make a point of listening to the programme to gauge the
style and format before deciding to submit an application. Some charities recruit one of their celebrity supporters to narrate the appeal;
others field someone who has benefited from the charity, e.g. a heart
attack victim appealing for the British Heart Foundation. There is
useful research data available from Radio 4 indicating what has
worked well previously.

You must give detailed thought to the response generated by the
appeal. This can be such an effective means of reaching potential
donors, because it is easy for the donor to respond and because it is
instant, you must be prepared for the volume of the response. If you
are using a national station, you will be well advised to use a telephone agency and the station may be able to help you in choosing the
right one. Remember, when your appeal goes out the responses will
probably all come at the same time while it is still fresh in the minds
of listeners.

2 Creating appeals

Radio stations depend on their ability to attract and retain listeners, so they concentrate much effort on identifying their listening audience and profile them accurately. If they fail to do this the station will not succeed. Local independent radio is heard by 55 per cent of the UK population each week. People listen because they enjoy the service and because the radio station is part of the local community. This is where local charities can capitalise on independent radio by proposing a fund-raising appeal in the local catchment area. This will involve local people and increase the profile and credibility value of the radio station.

Your appeal should be:

- relevant to the radio station, the catchment area and the listener profile;
- fun – your cause may be serious, but any appeal should capture the imagination;
- well thought out in terms of a mechanic. How does the appeal work and what is unique about it?
- well supported within the local community through your existing volunteers and donors. Will there be a local presence and activity coinciding with the broadcast? The greater the awareness the more attractive your appeal will be to the executives at the radio station.

Your approach is important, bear the following in mind:

- Have you actually listened to the radio station and are you familiar with its programme style and its presenters?
- Make contact with the programme controller, promotions or marketing manager or with a particular presenter. Try to contact them by telephone to arrange a meeting since they probably receive hundreds of letters each week and your application may be lost in the pile. If you have a relevant and well thought out proposal, your contact will be happy to find a new way to fill airtime with an attractive and appropriate item for the listeners.

To start you off, here are some ideas:

- A direct appeal for cash can work, but your message will need to be strong and you will be limited to a short burst appeal to avoid boring or alienating the listeners. Perhaps you could obtain free prizes to give away at intervals through the day, e.g. after so many calls pledging donations, the next lucky caller has their name put into a draw for a holiday prize.

- If you are prepared to put in a lot of work beforehand, auctions always work well; especially if they are themed to the prizes on offer, e.g. pop memorabilia. Auctions of promises or wishes are becoming increasingly popular and are not too difficult to organise. Some popular prizes are: trips in police helicopters; tours of the Houses of Parliament; driving round a racing circuit, etc. These are things that are not necessarily easy to buy, but they offer novelty value, and can be great potential for additional publicity. Why not offer dinner for two in unusual venues; an oil rig, an air raid shelter or in the middle of a roundabout!

- If you need gifts in kind to support your cause, appeal for these. For example, if you need to set up a night shelter for the homeless, draw up a shopping list of the necessary items for local people or companies to contribute.

- Appeals for items that can be turned into cash, i.e. used stamps, aluminium cans, petrol vouchers, etc, can form the basis of a collection from listeners.

- Do not forget the value of time; if you need volunteers, recruit them by radio appeal. If you are an environmental charity needing to clear a canal or a beauty spot, the right type of radio appeal can achieve this by asking listeners to volunteer a few hours of their time. You may even recruit active volunteer fund raisers.

Radio appeals are very competitive and you may find that a local radio station is not willing to run such a campaign free of charge. Some charities work with a commercial sponsor to develop their campaign and the radio station receives advertising revenue from the sponsor in exchange for running the appeal. Simple advance enquiries will indicate whether this is the preferred method for the radio station. If so, start with existing advertisers and the station may help you to put together a package if they like your idea.

3 Adoption

Some radio stations adopt a charity each year and channel all of their fund-raising activities towards that cause. Find out how they select the chosen cause and alert your volunteers to keep their antennae alert.

Television

Television appeals

(This area is covered by the Broadcast Appeal Consortium's Code of Practice, available from the Broadcasting Support Services)

Possibly the most difficult area to use for fund raising, since it is an expensive medium with few opportunities. The best known is the BBC1's *Lifeline Appeal*, which has a ten minute slot on one Sunday in each month. Any medium sized or large charity can apply for this slot through an established process. Details and criteria are available from the BBC and, because many charities do not consider this as an option, it is well worth trying. Other free television opportunities are limited; in the 1980s ITV launched the Telethon, but since the reorganisation of the networks, this has been disbanded and it is not likely to return. Events such as the 'Secret Policeman's Ball' and the 'Hysteria Concert' were created for particular causes. They provided entertainment as well as an opportunity to appeal to viewers. Creating these events requires knowledgeable people with experience and the ability to attract performers and market the concept and rights to an appropriate television company. Comic Relief continues from strength to strength and, in order to benefit from it, you should apply to Charity Projects (*see* useful address list in Appendix III) for grant details and an application form. Children in Need (*see* Appendix III for address) is the other successful television appeal, funding many children's projects across the UK; so apply for a grant if your work falls within their criteria.

The *Blue Peter* appeal is an example of a television programme that includes appeals at certain times of the year. Children are encouraged to collect a gift in kind and companies translate this into cash. Contact the programme researcher to find out whether you may be able to benefit. Ideas for the appeal format are also welcome; each year Blue Peter has to come up with a new format and means of raising cash from anything that has a resale or recycle value.

If your charity deals with aid or disaster relief for developing countries, you should research the Disasters Emergency Committee (DEC), who negotiate with the BBC and Independent companies to secure coverage for disaster appeals. The DEC is a recognised consortium of charities who divide all income for a particular disaster. It is very difficult to join this group, but it is possible to become an associate member if your cause falls within the general remit of the group; and your work in a particular country complements the project portfolio of the key member charities.

Beyond the above, the best possible way to build awareness for your charity through television is to gain news coverage. (See chapter 12 on 'Public Relations'.)

Television advertising

Since 1989, the UK's Independent Television Commission (ITC) has relaxed the rules to enable charities to advertise on television in the same manner as any commercial product; by buying time to advertise. Despite several years of this freedom, one rarely sees charities advertising regularly in the commercial breaks between programmes. This is because it is such an expensive medium and even those charities such as Save the Children, the NSPCC and the Samaritans who use this advertising technique restrict their appeals to irregular, off peak slots, sometimes only on an annual basis. Television advertising can be used to:

- raise funds
- recruit new donors
- promote membership schemes
- raise the profile of your charity or advertise a particular appeal.

If you have the financial resources to consider television as a medium, the quality of the advertisement will need to be high before you can even attempt to buy air time. Select an agency to handle everything; negotiating with the networks, creating the advertisement and producing the finished product. Many charities have tried this medium and failed expensively. Those who count the exercise a success applied the creative knowledge gained from successful direct mail campaigns and national press advertising. Some of the most successful televised charity advertisements have been based on direct mail packs. If a direct mail pack provokes the right response, it can probably be translated for television. Choose an agency that is familiar with fund raising and direct marketing for charities.

Extract from the ITC Code on advertising

Advertisements for charities should:

(a) handle with care and discretion matters likely to arouse strong emotions in the audience;

(b) not suggest that anyone will lack proper feeling or fail in any responsibility through not supporting a charity;

(c) respect the dignity of those on whose behalf an appeal is being made;

(d) not address any fund-raising message specifically to children;

(e) not contain comparisons with other charities;

(f) avoid presenting an exaggerated impression of the scale or nature of the social problem to which the work of the charity is addressed, e.g. by illustrating the message with non-typical, extreme examples;

(g) not mislead in any way as to the field of activity of the charity or the use to which donations will be put.

—————————— Telephone ——————————

The telephone is an integral part of everyone's life; so it is an ideal medium for fund-raising purposes. Telephone fund raising has received negative publicity in recent years, aligned to telephone sales. Before condemning it outright, however, consider why all major charities continue to use it and how your charity could benefit. If approached with care and sensitivity, this can be a successful way to raise funds. (The ICFM produce guidelines on telephone fund raising).

Uses of the telephone

Direct fund raising

Usually based on a list that the charity has built up from another activity (membership, campaigning, event attendance, etc); the people on the list, having already demonstrated their contribution to the cause, are contacted with information about the charity or a specific project and ways in which they could help. This is usually done with a carefully prepared script to guide the caller and anticipate a variety of responses. A positive response will be translated into a donation via a credit card, banker's order or a cheque via a letter following up the telephone call. Some charities make cold calls, but this is less effective and thus increasingly unpopular.

Thank you

The telephone can be effective when used to thank high value donors. Any gifts over £500 (or whatever you consider to be a large gift), should receive a call to thank the donor. This can be just as cost effective as a letter and the donor should be impressed with your level of service. Such a call can often prompt further support, not by a direct solicitation, but because the donor feels that their gift has been an important one. Some Directors of Fund Raising, or their equivalent, will select the top five to ten donors each day to call and thank them. This is a very successful activity.

Lapsed donors and supporters

A telephone call may be an effective way of re-establishing contact and reviving support. Even if it does not persuade previous supporters to give, it will provide useful information on what they think and why they decided to withdraw their support.

Volunteer and group member recruitment

Some charities use the local telephone books or electoral register simply to call people to ask them to join a group of local volunteers. I do not think this is particularly effective. It is better to start with a list of known supporters and asking them to recommend other possible volunteers, builds up a network for telephone calls. Always start your call by saying 'Mr/Mrs X suggested I call you since you may be interested in....'

Local businesses

The telephone is the lifeline for business, so it makes sense to use it to approach small and medium-sized businesses for support. Larger companies require a different approach (see Chapter 9). Charities have gained company sponsorship for specially tailored events, as, for example, a business balloon race where local companies are telephoned and asked to sponsor a balloon for £50 with the opportunity to win a case of champagne. If the event is tailored to telephone fund raising from small and medium-sized companies, it can be successful as well as cost effective. Although it is a method used by many charities, it can still be relevant when planning local appeals. The telephone is also a very effective means of selling advertising in event programmes, annual reports, diaries, year books, etc.

A word of caution; there are several commercial companies who will offer to undertake these telephone approaches on behalf of your cause. Look very carefully at their costs, terms and conditions and do take up references from any other customers. You should consider how a third party might use and promote your name before entering into any legal agreement for such a service. You must also ensure that such arrangements fully comply with the new Charities Act.

Response mechanism

The telephone is the obvious response mechanism for many of the fund-raising techniques mentioned throughout this book.

Responding to enquiries

If someone has shown an interest in your cause, why use a letter to respond to their enquiry? Why not ring to discuss their enquiry and answer their questions? You will learn more about your potential donor and you will have made the first step towards starting a relationship.

Research

No fund raiser can work in a vacuum, no matter how good you think your idea may be, you must first research what impact it will have on the potential donor. The telephone can be a vital tool for developing your planning and refining your ideas. Simple telephone research can be done in house, provided you have thought through the purpose of your approach, the questions you need to answer and how your are going to assimilate your responses.

TELEPHONE TECHNIQUES

In order to capitalise on these opportunities by using the telephone, you must absorb some of the basic telemarketing techniques. There are books available on this subject, but some key points for early practice and consideration are:

Prepare
- know who you are going to call, ideally you should have a name
- know the history of your prospect, what contact has the charity had before? with what results?
- know what you are going to say, use notes
- know what the likely questions or objections are, and have the answers ready
- have pen and paper ready to make notes.

Attitude and approach
- be confident and comfortable with using the telephone
- have a smile in your voice
- be positive.

Introduction
- make sure you are talking to the right person
- introduce yourself and your organisation
- say briefly what the call is about.

Be interesting and enthusiastic
- put yourself in their place
- describe the benefits, what is in it for them
- use their name
- react appropriately to what they say
- do not plough on regardless.

Ask the right questions (in the right way)
- closed questions will get you a yes or no answer, e.g. Did you enjoy the film?
- open questions will get you information, e.g. What did you enjoy about the film?
- summarise what has been said and agreed; this helps to confirm understanding, e.g. So you enjoyed the film because of the strong plot and excellent acting?

Listen
- empathise with your prospect; show that you understand how they feel
- pick up on clues as to what they are interested in, what concerns them, etc, and use this information to tailor your call.

Ending the call
- know when you have achieved your objectives and close the call
- know when you are not going to get what you want, is there an acceptable compromise position?
- whatever the result of the call, leave it on a positive note, even if you do not succeed, leave your prospect with a good feeling about you and your charity
- ensure you have all the information you need to follow up the call as required.

After the call
- record all the relevant information on the call and store it for the next time.

Telephone provider services

There are three main telephone services offered to fund raisers by British Telecom, Mercury and other service providers. All have cost implications and the first step should be to contact the marketing or sales departments of the appropriate companies.

Free phone

Usually prefixed by 0800 or 0500 dialling codes, this is simply a system for charging the cost of any call to the receiver, i.e the charity, rather than to the caller. This can encourage a greater response, but do consider all the cost implications before choosing this method.

Local call

Usually prefixed by a 0345 code and not as well know as the 0800 service. However, it is gaining greater awareness since the advent of telephone banking. This system charges the caller at the local rate regardless of the distance of their call. The remainder of the cost is charged to the charity receiving the call. People who know about this system will be more inclined to use it to call long distance during the working day to make their donation, and they will stay on the telephone longer. The cost of this service can also be quite considerable and it may be difficult to predict the benefits accurately, so investigate it thoroughly with the service provider before committing to it.

Premium rate lines

Originally prefixed with the 0898 code, they have now diversified into several other prefixes, e.g. 0891, etc, since the early lines gained a poor reputation in the market place. The costing is considerably more complex than any other service and will depend on how you choose to provide the service. A premium line provides you with an opportunity to get people to call in, and while they are on the line, there is an additional charge for the length of the call which is collected by the service provider and given to the charity. The most effective way to capitalise on this service is to use a specialist agency and a list of these can be obtained from the service providers. An agency will have the technology and the experience to manage the whole process for you.

Premium line rates can be very expensive for the donor, so you must have a strong proposition to encourage people to call. Charities often use this service to raise funds for a campaign, but without always considering that people may be reluctant to use these lines; parents may block children's access to them and the area has attracted adverse publicity.

Premium lines can be used very successfully when there is a desirable prize on offer and sufficient publicity to create a general awareness of the activity. One of the most successful uses of this service was to encourage voting for the Page Three Girl of the Year in the *Sun* newspaper, where the winner, chosen at random from the callers, went out to dinner with the winning girl. This may seem a trivial event, but it illustrates the type of interest and awareness you need to create to benefit from this technique.

11

TRUSTS AND FOUNDATIONS

'Approaching trusts is a game – and more like snakes and ladders than like chess.' – Trust Administrator.

Introduction

At first glance, the very existence of grant-giving trusts might appear to represent the answer to every fund raiser's dream – indeed, what other bodies have been established for the sole purpose of distributing specific sums of money to worthy recipients? While it is true to say that the hundreds, if not thousands (we cannot be sure of the exact numbers), of grant-making trusts that exist in the UK and abroad are a vital source of funding for charities, it would be incorrect to assume that the funds they provide are easy pickings. In fact, the only common bond that grant-making trusts really share is that they have usually been established to distribute grants according to an agreed and binding set of objectives.

Grant-giving, or charitable trusts are bodies established by individuals, companies or groups to distribute funds to charities and, in some cases, to needy individuals. These trusts are independent, with their own income operating within criteria set out by their funders and initial founders. A charitable trust is established with a group of trustees, usually assisted by an administrator or trust secretary; these people are responsible for assessing applications and distributing grants.

In the United Kingdom the Charity Commission has sought to ensure that grant-making trusts are open about the type of beneficiary they favour and the size of grants they give. The new charity accounting regulations and revised SORP (Statement of Recommended Practice), require disclosure of grants. Some trusts, however, still persist in keeping their activities private. Would-be applicants should, therefore, always bear in mind that, even if the trust's stated objectives appear to match their own exactly, there is no such thing as a dead cert trust application, although with careful research, attention to detail and patience, those endeavouring to obtain funding in this way are often rewarded.

Identifying trusts for approach

Grant-making trusts

These support a wide range of charities, both at national and local levels, so most charities can identify those to which they can apply. It can be hard work identifying trusts and researching their aims and criteria; some of the most responsive trusts may not appear in every list and directory.

Company trusts

These may either be directly attached to the company in question or be run independently of the company, but can usually be identified through company directories, such as the *Major Companies Guide,* published by the Directory of Social Change (DOSC). They are less secretive than other types of trust, and you will save time if your initial approach to such trusts is made via the telephone; most company Community Affairs co-ordinators would prefer to discuss their donation policies over the telephone, rather than be bombarded with wasted applications.

Other grant-making trusts

The Charity Commission can be a good place to find out about these. Most trusts are registered here, and details are held on computer files, in addition to the files and annual reports also available for inspection. However, it is necessary to visit the Commission, and to make an appointment to do so in advance if files are to be retrieved. It is often easier, therefore, to undertake initial research using one of the available directories of grant-making trusts. The Charities Aid Foundation's *Directory of Grant Making Trusts* is published every two years; the 1995 directory includes details of over 3,000 grant-making trusts in the United Kingdom. For further details on the country's top givers, the two volumes of *A Guide to the Major Trusts*, published by the DOSC, are excellent sources of information.

Thinking about approaches

Once you have identified trusts whose objectives will encompass what your charity is trying to achieve, build up a profile of each trust from the information available, i.e. correspondent (if the name is available), address, application deadlines, any application guidelines, past donations, size of resources, annual grants and geographical restrictions. From your research you should have a *hit list* of your top trust prospects and this should be circulated to your charity contacts, committees or trustees to ascertain whether they have further information or personal contact with the trustees. Local solicitors and bank managers often control local trusts not publicised elsewhere. Contacts are useful in any trust approach, but you should not consider them to be substitutes for a carefully thought out and professional approach.

How to write a good trust proposal

Develop a concise and clearly written proposal.

1   Summary

Gives an instant résumé of the identity of the charity, what your proposal involves and how much you are requesting.

2   Introduction

Describe your charity and its beneficiaries and why it differs from other bodies working in the same field. Keep this section brief and do not be tempted to go into great detail.

3   The need

Moving from the general to the specific, give details of the project, its cost and who it will benefit. Try to talk people rather than bricks and mortar.

4 Objectives

List these and how they will be measured.

5 Methods

Having stated your objectives, now describe how you will achieve your aims.

6 Budget

Although you have defined the sum you are requesting from the trust, you should also place this in the context of the whole budget (in a summarised version). The trust will wish to know how its donation will fit within the whole project, what other donors have given and whether the project is realistic in its expectations. Make clear whether you are seeking a single donation, a recurrent donation or an interest free loan. Future funding is also worth mentioning, particularly in a capital campaign to provide building funds, when the trust may want to know how running costs will be met.

7 Evaluation

Your objectives should be measurable, but assessment by an external body will lend further credibility to your application.

Although these seven stages should furnish all the information required by the trust, the whole document should be concise, preferably not more than three sides of A4 paper. Remember how competitive this area is and that some trusts receive several hundred applications for consideration at each trust meeting. Most secretaries and administrators will prepare a brief résumé of your proposal for the trustees, and your summary may form the basis for this. It is better to submit a short proposal communicating the key points to trustees. They can always ask for further information on any relevant aspect. Most trusts will expect to receive a copy of your latest accounts and an annual report when you submit your application.

Approaching trusts

Once your proposal is prepared and a target trust identified:

- check that your research has been adequate and that your proposal is appropriate to the trust;
- ascertain the dates for submissions by looking in the trust directory or by contacting the trust;
- typed presentations are much preferred to hand written proposals;
- check the name of the correspondent. Where a name is not given, address your application to the secretary or administrator;
- although some trusts discourage telephone contact, if this is not the case, it can be beneficial to check details and prepare the ground for your application;
- do not leave your request for funds open ended; specify the amount you require;
- only write to a handful of trusts at any one time and, if asked whether you are approaching other trusts, be open and honest. Administrators talk to each other and compare notes.

Conclusion

Trusts are a valuable source of funds for most charities, but they are not a short-term source; patience and persistence is needed. With many trusts you may not even receive a rejection notice. Try to build contacts and relationships with trusts and their executives. Most charities have a core list of trusts on whom they can depend; sometimes they do not even require a fresh application.

On receiving a grant, keep the trust informed about the progress of the project; this may even prompt further donations. Trusts rarely seek publicity, but they do like to know that their investment is being well managed.

Once you have gained experience in this field, you can extend your range by exploring foundations in other countries; again there are specialised textbooks and directories.

12

LEGACIES AND IN MEMORIAM DONATIONS

For many charities, In Memoriam donations are a major source of income. This depends to some extent on the cause, but several £ millions are donated to causes each year in memory of the deceased. Medical charities have always dominated this market, for obvious reasons, but, with a little effort, many other causes are now developing In Memoriam as a source of income.

As public awareness of your cause increases, you will probably receive unsolicited In Memoriam donations. To become pro-active in this field here are some suggestions for you to consider.

1 Place an entry in the local telephone books and Yellow Pages, since that is where people will search for local charities.
2 Make personal approaches, preferably through volunteers, to local funeral directors (there are over 4,000 in the United Kingdom), to give some basic information about your cause. Mailing funeral directors is not as effective as setting up meetings with local funeral administrators. Leave them with details about your organisation and ensure that they have a local contact name and address.
3 Small advertisements in the local press can be effective; reminding people of your existence and highlighting the importance of donations to your cause rather than floral tributes. They should incorporate all relevant registered charity information.
4 There are several major funeral organisations: the National Association of Funeral Directors (NAFD); CWS Funeral Services (Co-operative Society funeral directors); Funeral Standards Council; Funeral Planning Council. The NAFD holds annual con-

ferences and produces a monthly magazine, *Funeral Director*, in which you could place an advertisement. None of these organisations has set a route for charities wishing to approach them so you will need to seek an advertising opportunity, or a meeting to discuss how you may be able to promote your cause to their members.

Some local charities shy away from being pro-active in securing In Memoriam donations, but more are coming to accept that donations to charity in memory of an individual are now part of the funeral process.

Legacies

by Tom Smith, Smee and Ford Ltd

Introduction

Legacies can be an enormously important source of income for charities. The Battersea Dog's Home in London, for instance, derives 97 per cent of its voluntary income from this vital source. Therefore, legacy fund raising is a key area of potential income for your charity to consider. Whether your cause is local or national is not of fundamental importance. An average charitable Will contains three legacies and often large and small, local and national charities feature in it. Attracting people to support your cause through their Will is the key issue to be addressed later in this chapter.

A recent edition of the Charities Aid Foundation's *Charity Trends*, showed that legacy income to the top 500 charities in the United Kingdom was collectively valued at £521 million. This represented 32 per cent of all voluntary donations. While the top 500 charities includes all the household name charities, it would be unwise to jump to the conclusion that legacies end there. An increasing number of the medium and small charities are actively promoting legacies. Although it is impossible to say precisely how much goes to charities via legacies overall, one should look realistically at figures in excess of £800 million. Independent probate research carried out in 1993 concluded that 242,000 recently deceased residents of England and Wales with estates of £5,000 and over collectively left inheritances worth £16.5 billion.

Some of the language used in Wills can be confusing, it seems so far removed from everyday language, but a Will is no more and no less than a set of written instructions detailing what happens to all you possess (your estate), when you die. You can make as many as you wish, but the latest always supersedes any previous Wills. Additions or deletions can be made by means of a Codicil, and you can also make as many of these as you wish.

An executor is responsible for realising the deceased's estate, paying off any existing debts and distributing the remainder in accordance with the terms of the Will. Under English law, a maximum of four executors, who are usually a mixture of family, friends and professionals, can be appointed. The professionals most frequently used are solicitors, banks and accountants. From a strictly charity perspective, solicitors are viewed as the most important and are named as executors in 30 per cent of charitable Wills. It is advisable that potential executors are asked ahead of time if they are prepared to undertake the task.

A Will also needs to be signed, dated and witnessed. You must understand what you own and what you giving away, and two people must witness it. They are not permitted to benefit under the terms of the Will and both should be present when it is signed. Then they add their own signatures.

Three popular offers

A charity can appeal for three basic legacy types. These are specific, pecuniary and residuary.

1 The *specific* legacy is an item and can be valuable or valueless. On one hand it could be your home, a piece of land or an item of jewellery; or it could be an old paperback novel or second hand clothing.

2 The *pecuniary* legacy takes the form of a fixed cash sum. A survey conducted in 1993 revealed that the average pecuniary received by charities in the United Kingdom was valued at £1,700. The main advantage of this type of legacy is that they are easier to sell to a potential legator, who should understand the idea of leaving a particular sum to a charity. The main disadvantage is that, once the Will is made, the value of the gift begins to diminish immediately. The only sure method of protecting the value of a pecuniary legacy

is to have it index-linked in the Will or have it constantly up-graded through Codicils. This type of cash-based legacy is currently the most popular, with 52 per cent taking this form.

3 The *residuary* bequest (or legacy) is most sought after by charities involved in legacy promotions. In simple terms the residue means whatever is left over after all other gifts are paid. The residue can be divided into percentages or fractions and in some cases one charity can inherit the entire residue. The 1993 CAF survey (referred to above), also showed that an average share of residue was worth £20,600. The principal benefit to a charity inheriting such a gift is that, over time, the value should increase even if the Will is made, and left unchanged, many years prior to death.

Most charitable Wills contain three charitable gifts. These are usually a mixture of the various types of legacies and are spread on a fairly broad basis across the fund-raising spectrum. It is very rare for an individual to devote all of their legacies to one cause or area.

Reversionary bequests – the fourth offer

There is a fourth dimension to legacy giving. Those described above are the best known and promoted as outright gifts. A reversionary can take all of the above forms; specific, pecuniary and residuary. The significance being that they are delayed or deferred inheritances, payable only after the death of one or more persons, covering (in some cases) more than one generation.

In this event, it becomes apparent that charities will not receive their entitlement say until after the death of the last surviving grandchild of the Will-maker. The funds or assets are held in what are known as trust funds to provide income for the lifetime enjoyment of the life tenants.

If the ultimate charitable gift is a cash sum (pecuniary), it may be of little value when it matures. Conversely, with wise investment to secure capital growth, the reverse can happen. For example a reversionary residue bequest, where there has been no *resort to capital*, should be worth considerably more than when it was first bequeathed. However long these bequests take to mature, the charity, as the *remainderman*, must ensure that contact is maintained with the Trustees to safeguard the benefit.

From time to time, animals are made life tenants of trust funds. While this is legal, it can be bad news for charities. Some time ago an elderly woman from Lancashire left her £30,000 residuary estate upon trust for her tortoise, Fred, to enjoy the income for the remainder of its natural life. The ultimate beneficiary is a well known national animal charity. Fred was 36 years old when his owner died and he has a life expectancy of at least 100 years. The charity in question has got 64 years to wait!

Tax and charitable legacies

For the most part, charitable legacies are free of Inheritance Tax. They are also exempt from the imposition of Capital Gains Tax on assets such as stocks and shares inherited under a Will. To secure this benefit, the charity can either take on the assets by transfer or have them sold by the executors acting as *bare trustees* on their behalf. In the case of a residuary bequest, charities can reclaim any Income Tax deducted from interest earned during the administration period of an estate.

Legacy targeting

Research reveals many interesting facts about legacies. For instance, over 80 per cent (by number) of all charitable legacies are left by people whose estates were valued between £5,000 and £100,000. It also tell us that the average charitable female legator dies at the age of 82, while the average male charitable legator dies at 77. All the other people who make Wills without charitable mentions die, again on average some two years earlier! There must be some bizarre marketing message in the statement, but we have yet to see this reproduced in legacy literature and advertisements. Charitable Wills also take less time to mature than was thought several years ago, because the same research reveals that 51 per cent of these are made (or last updated), within three years of death. Two thirds of all charitable legacies are made by women, and charities involved in health and care issues are the most popular; arts organisations, at the other end of the scale, are the least.

From this profile it is implicit that most charitable legators are elderly, although not especially rich, and most legacies spring from the

Wills of women. It is therefore easy to assume that legacy promotion concerns seeking out and persuading the elderly to remember you in their Will. Modern charities, however, are actively involved in establishing relationships with their donors on a long term basis. Up to 70 per cent of all charitable legacies appear to come out of the blue, and charities have no idea of who the legator was and why they left the money. However, these are not fortunate accidents. People leave gifts for good reasons, and the events of a lifetime shape their opinions and preferences.

Charities target potential legators via many methods. Demographics and lifestyle profiling is being used increasingly by larger charities. Data on past legators is being used in conjunction with existing information on current donors and supporters. The ideal *lookalikes* can be propositioned either by direct mail or the telephone. Readership profiles can be ascertained to target legacy messages through the most effective media for a particular charity. At least one organisation for the blind and partially sighted has already advertised on radio. Communicating the Will-making or legacy giving message through video and audio tapes has been with us for several years, enabling charities to bring the topic into our homes. It has to be remembered that legacy promotion, on its present scale, has only been with us for fifteen years or so.

Promotional methods

Under the previous heading perhaps it appears that legacy promotions have become 'the appliance of science'. Not entirely. Many charities are still using the traditional methods with great success.

The important factor is to create awareness regarding your need for legacies amongst the people who you know best, your donors and supporters. A fulfilment device should be your absolute priority, preferable taking the form of a legacy leaflet or booklet (*see* under Legacy Literature — The Key Promotional Device, below). This free legacy literature can be promoted in your newsletter or you can run articles on the importance of making a Will and/or leaving a legacy. If possible, run a human interest feature on a recent legator and the importance of his or her final gift. The same method can equally well be applied to your annual report and accounts, and charities should take this advantage to illustrate legacy income received as a percentage of voluntary income. Separate space may be dedicated to commemorate the individual legacies received over a fiscal year. Do not be afraid to use innovative ways of displaying your need for legacies; one arts charity recently promoted legacies through its concert programmes. Other charities display their legacy materials (campaign posters, leaflets, etc.) at their main branch office and put them within easy access of the visiting public. This can be especially valuable at fetes, open days and events.

Your donations and covenant forms may be easily adapted to carry messages. 'Tick the box for your free legacy leaflet', or other similar messages should be integrated into as much promotional literature as appropriate. Several charities have included the tick box device on the reverse of donation envelopes. This makes response fairly easy and it is very inexpensive. Your materials should always take into account that some people suffer from inertia when it comes to returning items by mail, so, if practical, include the name and telephone number of your legacy advisor. Most of the above methods cost little to put into practice, except for the legacy literature.

Advertising for legacies has become commonplace. It takes two forms: advertising directed to the general public and advertising directed at the legal profession. The former is used mainly by household name charities using the offer of a free Will-making advice guide in the hope of recruiting potential legators. A few of these advertisements take up a whole or half page in the national press and specialist magazines, but most are 20 cm × 2 columns. You can expect to pay in the region of £2,000 to £4,000 for 20 cm × 2 columns space, but discounts are available if bought wisely. One large charity recently revealed that each positive response costs about £5. The legal professional format is the widest used. There are several appropriate publications and the largest contains around 2,000 individual charity entries. Make sure that they incorporate all relevant charity information.

Since Ken Burnett wrote his book *Relationship Fund Raising*, White Lion Press, a few years ago, a different mood has swept through the fund-raising world. Establishing relationships with donors and meeting their needs has risen in importance; perhaps to the extent that it should be considered a priority. Because the area of legacies is such a sensitive one, this would seem a logical approach and one national children's charity has recruited and trained local legacy advisors for this very purpose. Another children's charity, Barnardos, has been meeting its legators and prospects over many years, and this has become an established part of their fund raising culture.

Face to face fund raising for legacies may be planned or may occur as the result of a chance meeting. The following story was related to me recently by a colleague:

A well known national charity will eventually inherit a residuary bequest under the Will of the widow of a prominent London businessman. She made contact with the charity over the telephone after having seen a television programme featuring the services the organisation provides for children. After a lengthy initial conversation with the legacy officer, Mrs X said that, as a childless widow, she is now convinced that she has found the appropriate charity to eventually receive most of her large estate. To satisfy himself that Mrs X was happy with her decision, the legacy officer laid on a special trip for her and a close friend to visit a residential school run by the charity in the Home Counties.

Mrs X was deeply moved by the experience and praised the staff for their achievements with severely disabled children. When they left, she told the legacy officer that this experience had cemented her commitment to the cause and that it was her intention to make her Will as soon as possible. The following day, at her invitation, the legacy officer offered the names of several solicitors convenient to her home whom she could consult about her Will. Within days the Will was made by a solicitor of her choice, using the wording for the charitable bequest (on her instructions), provided by the legacy office. In effect, she has left the whole of her residuary estate to the school she visited, with the proviso that, if at her death, it no longer exists, the bequest can be used by the charity for some other comparable work.

Until he left the charity recently, the legacy officer kept in touch with Mrs X. He visited her regularly, telephoned her, sent copies of annual reports and Christmas cards. She has always maintained how happy she was that she had made her decision and that it gave her great peace of mind that her money would eventually help such a deserving cause.

There is a footnote to this story. In one of her many conversations with the legacy officer, she revealed that, sometime before she had seen the television programme, she had written to a well known hospital in London to discuss leaving them her money in her Will. To this day, she has not received a reply from the hospital.

Legacy literature — the key promotional device

Legacy literature takes two popular forms. Smaller organisations often use uncomplicated three-fold documents printed on A4 paper. Those with larger budgets frequently opt for a booklet or guide describing how to make or change a Will. There are a variety of formats used; some are bound within a cover while others are loose-leaf. Their objective is the same, however, to produce legacies for charities, although the booklet gives more space to cover certain issues in greater depth. Any material of course should make the all important *ask*. Some people regard legacy literature as too expensive, so you must put yourself in the position of the end user. Is your literature too glossy or not glossy enough? Is it all mission statement and not enough hard information? Try to balance the cost per copy with the likely response. Legacies, after all, at over £20,000 per average residuary are big money.

Putting your own legacy literature together is not difficult, but if your time is precious, there are many creative agencies on hand. If you choose to do it yourself, then conduct some research. There are many excellent examples of legacy literature available, so arm yourself with a selection, and you will discover useful tips. I recommend that you consider all of the following:

1 Brand your literature with the name of your charity and logo and other relevant registered charity information.
2 Devise an imaginative strapline, related to your cause if possible and do avoid 'Where there's a Will there's a Way'.
3 Include a paragraph on your charity and why you need the money.
4 Write in a warm and friendly tone of voice, avoiding legal jargon where possible.
5 Use colour illustrations and, perhaps, a dash of humour.
6 Ensure that the literature is reproduced in easy to read print size since most end users will be elderly.
7 Offer a variety of formats if relevant to your cause; i.e. large print, braille and audio tape.

8 Explain how to make and change a Will and the use of Codicils.
9 Cover the implications of intestacy, i.e what happens if you do not make a Will.
10 Explain the various legacy and bequest options, placing emphasis on residuaries.
11 Illustrate how a legacy or bequest to your charity should be worded in a Will.
12 Show actual examples of how recent legacies were able to benefit your charity.
13 Recommended that a Will be made professionally.
14 Show a case study of a legacy pledger and how a legacy was used to assist a member of your client group.
15 Gain endorsement from a well known celebrity.
16 Include the name and telephone number of your legacy advisor.
17 Include a pledge form or response device for obtaining further information.
18 Cross sell other fund raising methods offered by your charity, such as donations, covenants, give as you earn, etc.

Remember that your literature in itself is next to useless. It is no good having many hundreds of leaflets gathering dust in some storeroom. A pro-active legacy campaign must include strategies to put the literature into the hands of the decision makers, in this case your potential legators.

The role of the solicitor

It is often supposed by legacy fund raisers that the legal profession is quite influential in procuring legacies from clients making Wills. This is not really true. Those solicitors who do undertake probate work differ widely in their attitude towards advising their clients on the choice of particular charities, as was shown in the series of face to face interviews conducted some years ago with solicitors around the United Kingdom. Certain of them said that, when specifically requested by clients to express their views, they would state that particular charities were reputable, effectively run and deserving of support, some would proffer a charity handbook and suggest that the client made a choice, while others insisted that they would never recommend any charity. Some said that they had never been asked by their clients and yet others said that they were asked regularly.

Solicitors (and sometimes banks), do recommend discretionary charitable bequests to their clients, usually when a client cannot make up their mind about which charity to support. Although rare, such legacies bring in millions of pounds for charities each year, and frequently the solicitor will have tremendous influences as to which charities eventually benefit. A fund raiser for one charity recently approached the solicitor involved in a substantial charitable discretionary bequest under the Will of his late client. The fund raiser pointed out that the charity needed to build a new facility for their client group, and that monies received would be put to this use. The solicitor awarded the charity £500,000 from the estate and, in the fullness of time, the facility was completed. At this opening, the solicitor tearfully admitted 'I wish my client could have been here to see all of this.'

In practice, the majority of non-professional executors of Wills do engage a solicitor to carry out the administration on their behalf, although in this role, he or she has absolutely no influence over the contents of a Will. Despite this many charities buy advertising space in various annual charity supplements and legal journals. These are sent to all firms of solicitors and are used mainly for reference, but are rarely seen or read by members of the public. So do they work? There is no answer, but there must be some benefit when you consider that most of the larger charities agree that they cannot afford to stay out of these publications. Solicitors may use them, but it is unreasonable to expect them to sell your cause for you. Solicitors are also seen nowadays as actively promoting the Will-making ethos. On the one hand, we have the annual Make a Will Week, orchestrated by the Law Society, taking place each autumn and providing an excellent opportunity for charities to piggyback their marketing efforts on to it. Then there is Will Aid, a biennial event involving solicitors and promoted by six overseas aid charities with the added value of sponsorship by a major bank. The main thrust of both these promotions is to get more Wills made. This benefits everyone concerned: the public, the legal profession and, with one Will in seven being charitable, not least the voluntary sector.

Promoting the Will-making and legacy cultivation process has been taken a stage further by a firm of solicitors in Lancashire. With the aid of a video and accompanying Will-making kit, the firm seeks to work hand in hand with charities to make Wills on a wider basis. The demand for the Will-making kit and video will be generated by using the off-page advertising by charities promoting free legacy literature. Obviously the firm concerned cannot guarantee that legacies will be the end product, but at least a valuable service for each charity's responders is achieved. Each charity is to have the video badged with its own special legacy message.

Conclusion

This chapter is not a complete guide to legacies and fund raising. Issues that are important today may not be so tomorrow. Promotional methods will change as attitudes in society change. In the United Kingdom, in 1993, recently deceased people left a total of 72,000 legacies to various charities. Additionally, there were a further 12,000 legacies left to places of religious worship, including churches of all denominations, synagogues and mosques. These produced a total estimated income in excess of £800 million. Just suppose that there were 100,000 legacies a year!

Legacies are affected by the financial climate. In 1988, the average residuary in the United Kingdom was worth £25,000 and has fallen in value since then. Fortunately, however, analysis shows that, since 1988, we have experienced a steady growth in legacy numbers year on year. In that respect, legacy awareness and marketing is working.

Legacy success should not always be viewed solely in terms of income; the numbers of legacies are important too. Remember that it is never too late to become involved in legacy fund raising; there is a constantly recurring market. Approximately 1,000 new Wills are made each day in the United Kingdom, affording that amount of new fund-raising opportunities. With only one Will in seven at the moment having a charitable element, it can be seen clearly that we still have some way to go.

Making legacies the popular method of giving is in the hands of charities and their fund raisers. Despite claims from some quarters, there is no evidence to suggest that legacies suppress income from other forms of fund raising. One fund raiser said that he regarded legacies as 'the ultimate late big gift campaign'. I think that this is a fair statement. Could you, for instance, give a charity over £20,000 now?

13
STATUTORY FUNDING

Considerable amounts of money are available for charities and other voluntary organisations from statutory sources; in the United Kingdom this comes to around £4 billion and is rising. So it is well worth investing some time and effort in exploring these avenues. The main sources are:

- central government
- local authorities
- quangos (quasi non government organisations)
- European Union.

The advent of the National Lottery will also provide further funds for voluntary organisations.

The funds are available as grants, contracts, loans, reliefs (e.g. tax reliefs) and the use of office space, personnel and equipment. To access statutory funds you need to:

- research the area thoroughly, know what is available, from where and for what;
- identify the key people at the appropriate department and work to develop a good relationship and understanding of them;
- persevere, it can be a long and often laborious process.

A successful application for statutory funds requires a thorough review and analysis of the organisation. Can it be classified as local, regional, national or international? Define the areas of work in which the charity operates and outline its aims and objectives. A detailed analysis will enable you to target your request for support as accurately and appropriately as possible. It is also worth considering the areas in which the charity would not be happy to work, since some statutory funds come with very specific restrictions.

Central government

The majority of funds given by central government are for core funding and administrative costs and are given to national organisations or at least national projects.

Funds are usually given where:

- the service provided by the voluntary organisation is preferable to statutory service;
- the voluntary organisation can provide appropriate competition or an alternative to the established statutory service;
- the voluntary organisation can enhance or complement the statutory service provided.

Many different government departments have funds available, so it is important to ensure that your are approaching the most appropriate one for your needs. Before making an application you should contact the department by letter or telephone to ascertain as much information as possible regarding the type of funds available, the main criteria for support and any other specific information, such as the best time of year to apply or the best format for the application.

Some of the main UK government departments to consider are:

- The Department of the Environment (especially through its Urban Programme)
- The Overseas Development Administration (ODA)
- The Department of Education
- The Department of Employment
- The Department of Trade and Industry
- The Department of Health
- The Department of Energy
- The Home Office.

If you find that these are not appropriate to your particular cause, investigate other departments who may not have such a large budget but who may have a closer affinity to your need, e.g. the Scottish or Welsh Office, Northern Ireland, Transport, etc.

The key to securing funding from these sources is through the 2P principle: Patience and Perseverance.

Quangos (Quasi Autonomous Non-Governmental Organisations)

These organisations are established by central government to work in specific areas and to a particular remit. Some examples of quangos are: The Arts Council, The Nature Conservancy Council and The Commission for Racial Equality, and they operate along much the same lines as the government departments.

Local authorities

Local and health authorities provide considerable amounts of funding and support for local projects and services. Because of this, developing a good relationship with the appropriate people and keeping them informed of local public feeling and opinion can often bring dividends for a charity. Support from local authorities, as from other statutory bodies, can come in many forms, ranging from grants to donation of premises. Local authorities are responsible for education, transport, housing, leisure and social services.

European Union

There are 15 member states comprising the European Union (EU). For fund-raising purposes, you should think of the EU as divided into four key areas:

1 European Commission (EC)
2 Council of Ministers
3 European Parliament
4 Advisory Committees.

Considerable sums are available to support areas identified by the EC as meriting help. Some of the main areas are: AIDS in developing countries, anti-drug policies, disaster relief, education, the environment, ethnic minorities, food aid, immigrants, human rights, international youth projects, research, unemployment and women and development. Many grants are given on a joint funding basis which requires a matched amount from the project's home country. Funding applicants stand a better chance of success if they are truly international and cross border, as well as being high profile projects.

It is important to identify the most appropriate budget for your project; follow the correct submission procedure, and adhere to the submission deadlines. This is a complex, time consuming and frustrating area from which to solicit funds. You will certainly have a greater chance of success with the support of someone who has practical experience of the processes involved. Some large charities now have staff in Brussels solely to negotiate this area on their behalf. It is also vital to develop good relations with the various European Union people based both in the UK and in Brussels.

Further advice and information

There are many useful books available on statutory funding, and below I have listed some of the main sources of advice and guidance:

The Voluntary Services Unit (at the Home Office)

The National Council for Voluntary Organisations (NCVO)

The Directory of Social Change.

Other charities

Some charities do give grants to projects and organisations working in their area of specific interest, although grants will only be provided according to strict criteria. The best starting point is to make an initial contact with the appropriate charity to ascertain their preferred way of application and to obtain any other helpful information.

14

BIG GIFT AND CAPITAL CAMPAIGNS

Fund raising can hardly be described as a science, except possibly in the area of big gift fund raising, which is 80 per cent research and 20 per cent fund raising. Many of the United Kingdom's great institutions, historic buildings and hospitals have at some time had elements funded by a Big Gift Fund Raising (BGF) campaign. *In very simple terms this is a fund-raising technique that proves and agrees a financial need; then brings together a small core of people who believe in the need and are able to make a notable contribution towards it; who then identify other possible donors who may share their view; over 50 per cent of any fund-raising target in this area will come from less than 10 per cent of the donors.* Basically, you are trying to achieve your target quickly and economically by obtaining a few large gifts. BGF is a detailed process with several stages to success. This section can only give you a broad outline of what may be involved and, while it may help you in your review of fund-raising techniques available for any particular project, I would generally recommend that you seek practical experience and guidance in the area of BGF. This type of fund raising is about person to person giving, usually in face to face situations and the fund raiser's role is to organise and facilitate the whole process, controlling it at each stage and keeping it on track.

Getting started

If you or your governing body believe that you have an appeal that may be suited to attracting major gifts (five figures plus), and that you may have some idea of an audience capable of these gifts, either captive, i.e. already associated with your cause, or at least identifiable, the first step must be a complete review of your project and the possible funding sources. The three key steps of BGF must be considered fully from the outset:

1 Education: what is your project and what is the solution? You will need a strong, proven case statement in order to attract support.
2 Planning: what is the business plan to achieve the objectives behind your project?
3 Organisation: who are the people behind the plan who are capable of making it happen? Can you identify one donor to give £500,000 to start you off? Can you reach that person in a way that makes it hard to say no?

Campaign study and audit

These could follow the following structure:

External environment

1 Local demographics
   (a) Population
   (b) Housing
   (c) Wealth
   (d) Employment
   (e) Age profile.
2 Local industry profile
   (a) Major employers
       (i) type of industry
       (ii) employee numbers
       (iii) location
       (iv) relation to national companies
   (b) Does your organisation rate as a local employer?
       (i) number of employees
       (ii) local supplier
       (iii) properties
   (c) Trade associations
   (d) Historical industry profile (where relevant).
3 Geography
   (a) Main conurbations
   (b) Population division
   (c) Communication network, motorways, etc.
4 Local government
   (a) Key councillors

(*b*) Political bias

(*c*) Structure (City v County)

(d) Policies.

5 Local Media

(*a*) Radio

(*b*) Television

(*c*) Local papers

(*d*) Local magazines.

6 Leisure facilities

(*a*) Sport

(*b*) Arts

(*c*) Education

(*d*) Organisations and associations.

7 Competitor analysis

(*a*) Recent appeals

(*i*) techniques used

(*ii*) results

(*iii*) time period

(*b*) Ongoing fund raising

(*i*) prominent charities

(*ii*) local groups

(*c*) Evaluation of external environment.

Internal environment

1 Profile of your organisation's activities in area

2 Your organisation's unique selling points

3 Review of fund-raising activities to date

4 Current budget expectations

5 Future fund-raising proposition

(*a*) Case statement, establish the need and create the donor proposition

(*b*) Campaign objectives required to meet the case statement need.

Technique option review

1 Review all practical fund-raising techniques against:

(*a*) Suitability to achieve case statement

(*b*) Resource requirement (time and financial)

(*c*) Payback ability

(*d*) Suitability to region and external environment

2 Prioritise suitable techniques

(*a*) SWOT against case statements

3   Resources recommendations
4   Operating budget (preferably three years)
5   Timings.

Materials

1   What materials are required? e.g. campaign brochure, direct mail, etc:
    (a) Costs — sponsorship potential
    (b) Quantities
    (c) Timing
    (d) Responsibilities (in house v agency)
2   Separate identity and logo.

Public relations

1   Develop strategy in relation to external environment, case statement, opportunities and fund-raising plan:
    (a) Resources (in house v agency).

Overall campaign recommendations

1   To include:
    (a) Primary and secondary objectives
    (b) Evaluation and review criteria
    (c) Overall budgets (income and expenditure)
    (d) Overall timetable.

The biggest weakness of many ventures into BGF is the need itself. It must be proven and stand up to detailed review; many of the people you approach will be from the business community and they will review your appeal as they would any business investment, assessing its viability and efficiency.

From such an audit, you should be able to establish a budget for your project, timetable, endorsement by any other bodies and your initial fund-raising plans. This should provide a report to your governing body for their approval and involvement; motivating them to maintain their support for your cause.

Although the initial study can be carried out by the fund raiser, it is usual to form a study group from people already associated with the project and any interested parties who may be able to give a leading gift to the campaign. This group should not have more than eight members.

Planning group

When you have completed your study, proved the need and gained support from all the concerned parties, you need to form a group of people who will turn the study into a fund-raising plan. In other words, how to make it all happen? Ideally, those people who have supported you so far in the study group and the governing body may be suitable to form this core group. If not, your study will have highlighted individuals who will fit the bill. They do not have to be capable of giving at the very highest level, but they must have the ability to influence others and possess local knowledge and credibility. This group will help to identify financial leaders and they will bring together the fund-raising group who will make things happen. The essential element in this process is research, and then more research!

Remember that this technique is about people and face to face approaches. A core of people who have the necessary power and influence to enable them to approach your target donors for a gift. Once a person has been persuaded to give to the best of their ability, they will then go forth and persuade their peers to follow their example. Form your list of prospects by asking your planning group to contribute the local information enabling you to research and rank your prospective donors. You will also need to carry out desk research on suitable individuals, using all available reference sources. This is a more difficult process than it sounds and takes considerable time and attention to detail, especially when it comes to selecting those who will become your top level prospects for major gifts. You will also need to research how one person may be connected to another in some way.

The key sources for your list of possible contacts are:

- industry and commerce
- individuals
- professions
- trusts and foundations
- statutory organisation
- previous givers to an appeal
- board members and trustees.

Consider all of these categories at local, regional and national level, depending on the nature of the appeal. Each of the sources will also have its own sub-categories, i.e. industry and commerce can be broken down into finance, engineering, retailing, pharmaceutical, etc.

You should now be able to select the top six prospects and decide on a fail-proof way of approaching them. By ranking them in order, you create a wish list for filling the post of chair of your fund-raising committee, since you have now reached the stage where such a committee will consist of the people who will lead by their own donations and encourage their peers to help to achieve the target.

The fund-raising group

It is unlikely that you will reach this stage without at least six months of solid research and preparation. It is important to understand the patterns of giving and, although they may initially seem too technical and difficult to absorb, it is worth remembering that they have evolved from many years of successful BGF carried out by the most famous appeals. There is no right or wrong pattern, but common sense will dictate the best one for a particular appeal. Experience has shown that the major part of any appeal target will come from a few gifts or grants and not the broad, scatter shot appeal to the general public; 80 per cent of the money will be raised from less than 100 donors. Many of your large gifts will come in the from of covenants where income is received over a four year period. Gift Aid should also be encouraged, although donors may prefer to spread their payments.

Gift pattern examples for £500,000

Model 1			Model 2		
No of gifts	£	Total	No of gifts	£	Total
1	£60,000	£60,000	1	£60,000	£60,000
1	£50,000	£50,000	1	£40,000	£40,000
2	£40,000	£80,000	1	£30,000	£30,000
2	£30,000	£60,000	2	£25,000	£50,000
4	£15,000	£60,000	3	£20,000	£60,000
8	£10,000	£80,000	4	£15,000	£60,000
10	£5,000	£50,000	6	£10,000	£60,000
20	£3,000	£60,000	10	£4,000	£40,000
			25	£2,000	£50,000
			50	£1,000	£50,000

£500,000 from 48 people/organisations	**£500,000 from 103 people/organisations**

The two charts illustrate how the theory of BGF can work in practice; your planning group and fund-raising group will need to assess which of these or any other pattern will suit your needs and is achievable, given the case statement and the donor audience.

Whichever pattern you choose, your chair should be giving in the number one gift position to ensure they have sufficient inviting power to secure the other necessary gifts to complete the appeal. Having donated their own gifts, your fund-raising group will now endeavour to enlist other donors, following these five stages:

1 Identify
2 Inform
3 Interest
4 Involve
5 Investment (gift).

There are two ways to enlist people, either by bringing a group of individuals to hear a well presented proposal at a meeting when the chair will invite others to join; or by one to one meetings between members of the group and their contacts. The first method is risky since it is easier to decline when in a group. Enlistment meetings require careful planning and orchestration, but they are extremely effective within a short time span (stages 2 and 3). The meeting is not the time to ask for or to accept gifts, but the chair and the fund-raising group should follow up the meeting with a letter to each guest seeking to confirm their further involvement (stage 4); to invite them to the next group meeting and to arrange an individual meeting with their original contact to discuss their commitment (stage 5 which is their investment in the project).

Remember, money or property raised for a specific appeal can only be used in support of that particular appeal. Therefore, you need to:

- Plan very carefully
- Phase all appeals in the least specific manner
- Include flexibility in all appeal literature, e.g. 'Any additional funds raised from this appeal will be used in the furtherance of our general charitable purposes'.

These requirements are contained in Section 15.3 Part II of the Charities Act 1992.

As the fund-raising group grows and broadens into some of the middle ranging donations, it should start splitting up into sub-committees to target specific sectors and groups of individuals.

When you achieve in excess of 75 per cent of your final target, you may need to move away from the strict structure of BGF and broaden your approach through wider public exposure, even a public launch. Your activities up to this point have been relatively low profile and classified as the private fund-raising phase of any appeal. Now it is time to engage all the techniques outlined in this book to make the final push for the target.

Success in BGF is due to:

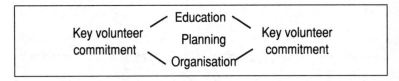

15

FURTHER FUND-RAISING TECHNIQUES

Membership schemes

These are schemes whereby people become members or friends of a particular charity, usually by paying an annual subscription. There are schemes for children, adults, families, organisations and companies, all offering benefits to both members and charity alike. Some membership schemes carry certain constitutional rights for members, such as voting at the AGM, but many are merely offering association with the charity. There are some very large and successful schemes, such as those run by the National Trust and the Royal Society for the Protection of Birds.

To set up a membership scheme from scratch requires considerable resources of time and money, but if the research has been done thoroughly and the charity has the right kind of benefits to offer, they can be useful and successful for a charity. Once a scheme has been established it needs to be serviced effectively and efficiently. The charity must deliver what it has offered its members within an acceptable time frame. Before such a scheme is launched, the ongoing manpower resources must be carefully considered.

Benefits to the organisation

Probably the main reason for an organisation to run a membership scheme is to develop and increase loyalty amongst its donors by developing a relationship with them to ensure their continued support and interest. But there are many other benefits to an organisation running such a scheme:

- it is a means of telling people about the organisation and its activities and thereby enhancing its profile and PR;
- it can be used as a source of volunteers and also as a means of thanking volunteers and acknowledging their achievements;
- it can create publicity for issues and elicit support for campaigns;
- it can be used to promote and publicise events that are being organised by and for the charity;
- it can be used to enhance specific appeals;
- it can attract corporate support and sponsorship;
- the size of the scheme can be used to demonstrate the volume of public support enjoyed by a charity, and this in turn can influence potential donors, grant makers, decision makers, etc.

Benefits to members

Anyone deciding to become a member of a charity or other voluntary organisation will have an interest in or feel an affiliation to that particular charity or cause. The charity must do all it can to maintain and develop that interest and ensure that members feel that they belong to the charity. To do this it is vital to keep them informed and updated. The best way to do this is to produce a regular newsletter for your members.

Other benefits can be offered to members. Exactly what these are will depend on the specific charity and the area in which it is involved but the type of benefits to consider are:

- access to facilities and properties belonging to the charity;
- free or reduced entry fees and priority booking for events and activities run by the charity;
- free or reduced rates for publications and merchandise produced by the charity;
- creating opportunities to meet with other members;
- branded merchandise, e.g., lapel badges and car stickers;
- access to events exclusively for members;
- access to a telephone advice or information line.

An exclusive and dedicated telephone number on a membership card can make a donor feel valued and important to the charity, even though such a telephone service is rarely used by members.

Pricing

This is a crucial factor to consider as you do not want to price your membership too high and deter people from joining, but you also need to achieve an appropriate level of income to ensure that the scheme is not too costly for the charity to administer.

Research what similar schemes are charging and consider what you are able to offer your members when deciding on the cost of membership. Most schemes elect to go for a reasonably low subscription rate, viewing it as a long term investment since it will encourage an ongoing relationship with the member that is likely to yield other donations and support. For example, the Imperial Cancer Research Fund in the United Kingdom established membership schemes for their regional units. Marketed as 'partners' schemes, they charge members a nominal £25.00 per annum in exchange for two newsletters per annum, a lapel badge or key ring and an annual tour around the unit.

The majority of membership subscriptions are paid by direct debit or covenant (with this method of payment, tangible benefits of membership should not exceed 20 per cent of the value of the subscription), which contributes to the long-term nature of the commitment and should be encouraged. It is possible to use honorary membership as an acknowledgment or reward for particularly outstanding outstanding support of the charity.

Schemes you may consider

Children's clubs

Many charities classify children as a prime area for fund raising and as a key target group to educate and inform about their cause; after all they are the donors of tomorrow. If your charity is suitable, you should certainly consider a junior club or membership scheme. These need to be administered in the same way as any other scheme, but the component parts need considerably more imagination, flair and fun. It is also useful to divide children into three age groups: 4–7, 8–12, 13–16. This is not to say that you need three separate membership schemes, but if you use the same scheme across the complete age range you will need to encompass material that will have universal appeal. You should consider a newsletter with cartoons, illustrations and competitions; badges are always popular; stickers; the right celebrity endorsement; incentives; opportunities to be involved and to do something; and above all the package must be interesting, and in keeping with current youth trends.

A mascot is a useful tool, particularly with younger age groups, especially if it translates into a cartoon character, soft toy and possible character costume for events.

Newsletters and all aspects of children's schemes must at all times be appropriate to the age profile of the membership, as should the cost of membership. Running this type of scheme effectively can be costly and time consuming, therefore this is a prime area for possible commercial sponsorship, provided you can establish a large enough membership base within your target audience.

Company membership

All of the benefits of membership schemes outlined above can equally apply to companies, but you need to adjust your thinking slightly. If you are a local charity there is no point approaching companies on a national scale. You should concentrate on local and possibly regional companies who will be more sympathetic to your cause and able to relate to your need.

One of the most effective elements to introduce to such a scheme is that of a membership logo that can be reproduced as a window sticker for retailers, an ordinary sticker for use on vehicles and other surfaces and reproducible on company literature and letterhead. This simple mechanic enables a local company to demonstrate to their consumers that they are active in supporting local charities. A similar principle has been used successfully for years by Rotary Clubs and Round Tables. Displaying such a logo can also act as a useful defence shield to other charitable appeals!

If you are not able to offer other tangible benefits to companies, think of ways that you may be able to help or involve their employees. In order to price such schemes effectively you may like to develop a pricing structure commensurate with the number of employees in the company, e.g. 1–10 employees £125, 11–50 employees £300, 50+ employees £500. It is important not to undersell yourself to companies so before developing such a scheme refer to the fuller chapter on corporate giving.

Event participants

If your organisation runs a large number of events, for example of a sporting or black tie nature, then you may wish to consider a special membership for participants or ticket purchasers. Usually such schemes are offered free as a way of keeping in touch with key supporters, unless you are able to offer a range of additional benefits such as merchandise, discounts, advance bookings, etc, when a subscription should be payable.

An established membership base in any of the aforementioned categories can be an extremely valuable asset of the charity in terms of further fund raising through cross-promotional opportunities. Through negotiation with appropriate companies, you can develop promotional offers to your membership which will not only be perceived as an exclusive benefit of membership, but should also provide profit on the transaction for the charity, e.g. a rose bush offer from a local nursery at £6.99 with a built in £1 donation to the charity (*see* Chapter 14).

———————— Lotteries ————————

With the advent of the National Lottery, interest and awareness in lotteries in the United Kingdom has never been higher. In 1993 the new National Lottery Act came into force, amending the law governing various forms of lottery contained in the Lotteries and Amusements Act 1976.

This is a complex area where you need to ensure that you are complying precisely with the law and, since certain types of lottery must be registered with local authorities, whereas others do not not require registration, lottery organisers must take their responsibilities in this area seriously. The Gaming Board for Great Britain should be your first point of enquiry, since they produce useful literature that will guide you through the types of lottery and the necessary registration and guidelines for each type. *Do allow plenty of time for this procedure*. The Gaming Board can also advise you on how a lottery differs from a competition. You can obtain a comprehensive code of practice for lottery organisers from the ICFM.

What is a lottery?

A lottery is the distribution of prizes by chance where the persons taking part, or a substantial number of them, make a payment or consideration in return for obtaining their chance of a prize.

Types of lottery

Small lottery

These are run at fêtes, dances, dinners, sporting events and other similar entertainments. They are legally classified as exempt entertainment. Such lotteries do not have to be registered, but the following regulations apply:

- no more than £250 can be spent on prizes;
- no monetary prizes;
- the lottery must be incidental to the event and not the main attraction;
- tickets can only be sold at the event and the results must be declared at the event;
- the profit from the lottery must not be used for private gain;
- if you wish to offer alcoholic prizes, you should obtain an Occasional Liquor Licence from the local Trading Standards Office and ensure that you do not sell tickets to people under 16 years of age.

Small lotteries are ideal for charity events since they are relatively easy to organise. Try to get all of your prizes donated, making them as attractive as possible, and make sure that you ask suitably extrovert people to promote the lottery on the day.

Private lotteries

These do not have to be registered, since they are intended for a society or group of people, not connected with gambling, who either work or reside on the same premises. The key restriction being that the lottery cannot be promoted outside the premises of the group or organisation taking part. Bear in mind that you should:

- only advertise the lottery at the premises in which the persons for whom the lottery is being promoted reside or work and, of course, on the tickets;

- use all proceeds for the purposes of the group or society promoting the lottery. Stationery and printing costs may be deducted;
- fix the price of the tickets, i.e. you cannot offer six £1 tickets for £5. The ticket must state who the promoter is and to whom the tickets may be sold. Tickets cannot be sent by post;
- tickets must display the name of the benefiting charity and the registered charity number;
- ensure that the promoter is authorised by the governing body of the benefiting society or group.

These are slightly more complex than small lotteries, but still relatively straightforward and very worthwhile when trying to raise funds in the circumstances outlined above.

Society and local authority lotteries

These are the major categories of lottery used to raise charitable funds by institutions, clubs, organisations, etc. Local authorities use them to raise funds for their normal expenditure. The starting point should be to register with the appropriate local authority and, where the value of the tickets put on sale for a single lottery exceeds £20,000 (or £250,000 in any one year from several lotteries), the society or local authority must register with the Gaming Board. If you intend to operate the lottery within this category, you must get the relevant details from your local authority and the Gaming Board in order to ensure that your registration is correct and complies within the law.

— The A to Z of fund-raising ideas —

A

Abseil
Adopt-A-
 (Scientist/Animal/Child,etc)
Aerobics (Sponsored/Marathon)
Air flights; balloon, plane, hang-
 glider, etc
Air miles
Angling competitions
Antiques Roadshow
Archery competition
Aromatherapy evening
Art auction
Assault course
Auction
Australian evening

B

Baby competition
Balloon race
Barbecue
Barn dance
Beard shave
Bed push
Beer race
Bike ride
Bingo
Blind Date competition
Board game marathon
Book hire
Book sales
Bowling competition
Bridge tournament
Bring and buy sale
Bungee jumping
Burns night
Bus pushing/pulling
Buy-A-Brick

C

Cake stall
Calendars
Calligraphy evening
Car boot sale
Car pushing
Car washing
Caribbean night
Carnival
Carol concert
Carol singing
Casino evening
Chariot race
Charity cricket match
Chess tournaments
Church collections
Clairvoyant evening
Clay pigeon shooting
Coffee mornings
Cold custard bath
Concerts
Cookery demonstration
Craft fair

D

Dance
Dance Till You Drop
Darts tournament
Debate evening
Dieting
Dinner dance
Disco
Dog walk/show
Donkey races
Duck race

E

Easter egg hunt
Egg eating

Egg & spoon races
Equipment hire
Exhibition adoption

F

Family fun day
Fancy dress party/hire
Fête
Fifties night
Film premiere
Fireworks evening
Flower festival
Football competition
Foreign coins
Forfeit night
French evening
Fun run/walk

G

Games evening
Garden party
Give As You Earn
Golf competition
Graphology evening
Greyhound racing
Gymkhana

H

Haircuts - sponsored
Halloween party
Harvest festival
Head shave
Horse show
Horseless trials
Hospital radio requests
House to house collection
How far?
How heavy?
How long?
How many?
How much?
How often?
How quick?

How slow?
Hypnotist evening

I

Ice skating
Inflatables (bouncy castles)
Initiative race
Irish bingo
Italian night
Its A Knockout

J

Jail break (Jail 'N' Bail)
Jam making
Jazz festival
Jewellery party
Jogging (sponsored)
Joke book
Jumble sale

K

Karaoke night
Keep fit
Kidnap (ransom money to
    charity)
Kipper eating competition
Knit-in
Knockout
Krypton Factor style contest

L

Lands End to John O'Groats
Late for work donations
Legacies
Lilo races
Litter cleaning
Local history evening
Lottery
Lucky dip
Luncheon clubs

M

Make up sessions
Marathons
Masked ball

Massage nights (!)
Mediaeval banquets
Mile of silver/copper coins
Milk float race
Model making/displays
Mountain climbing
Multi-activity day
Murder mystery parties
Musical concert

N

Nativity plays (schools)
Nature trails
Naughty but nice (cream cake
    eating)
New Years Eve party/New Year
    pledge
Night at haunted house
Non uniform days/mufti day
Non-talent contest (worst con-
    tender!)
Nougat eating
Nursery rhyme quiz

O

One hundred clubs
Open days at unusual places
Open gardens
Open house
Opera night
Orienteering
Outward bound day

P

Paint balling
Pancake race
Pantomime
Paper aeroplane competition
Parachuting
Parties
Pavement art
Petrol coupon collections
Pie & pea supper

Plant a tree
Plant sale
Polo day
Pop concert
Pram races
Promise auction
Pub crawls
Pub quiz
Puppet show

Q

Quaser Laser
Question of Sport
Question Time *viz* Radio 4
Quilting day or competition
Quiz night
Qwerty competition - speed
    typing

R

Race night
Raffle
Raft race
Rally driving challenge
Raves
Recipe book
Record breakers
Recycling aluminum cans
Rugby match 7s
Runs

S

Safari suppers
Sale of work
Santa's groto
Scavenger hunt
Sheep racing
Silences
Silent auction
Sing along
Sixties theme night
Sky diving
Slimming challenge

Slug racing
Softball competition
Spelling competitions
Static box
Student fund raising
Sun flower growing
Swimathon

T

Talent competition
Tea dance
Ten pin bowling
Toga party
Tombola
Toy fair
Toy library
Treasure hunt
Triathlon
Trivial Pursuits evening
Tug of war

U

UK and Ireland Corporate
   Games
Ukele concert
Underground race (London,
   Newcastle, Glasgow)
Underwear party
Unicycle race
Unwanted items sale

V

Valentine's day cards
Valentine message party
Vanishing lunches
Variety performance
Vegetarian evening
Vehicle push

Victorian day
Village fete
Vintage car rally

W

Walks
Watersport day
Weight of cake
Wellie throwing
Whelk eating
Whist drive
Wine tasting and auction
Wishing well
World's greatest/biggest/worst
   (vegetable/tie/T-shirt)

X

Xmas (Advent) calendar
Xmas evening/carols, mince
   pies/etc
Xmas fair
Xmas party
Xylophone concert

Y

Yacht racing
Yard of ale
Yellow Brick Road treasure hunt
Yo Yo competition
Yodling competition
Yoga day

Z

Zebra racing (people in cos-
   tumes)
Zimmer-frame racing
Zither concert
Zodiac evening

—— Face-to-face fund raising ——

There are many management books and training courses about developing this skill. We do it every day without thinking and it moulds our relationships and the way people perceive us. Problems arise when the communication process takes place in a formal setting and the individual needs to negotiate effectively on behalf of their cause, and gain a positive response from their audience; whether it is one person or one hundred.

It is not necessary to be an extrovert, but you must develop an awareness and honesty about your own ability to present all levels and in various circumstances. Identify suitable training courses to hone these skills; at least seek specialist knowledge from relevant books.

Here are some guidelines to help you in presenting effectively:

The objectives

- know why you are making the presentation and what you want to achieve. This will dictate many factors in your presentation, so keep it in mind throughout your planning and preparation, and in the presentation itself.

You

- consider the impact on your audience of your appearance and plan what you will wear. Make sure you feel comfortable. Do not wander about or hide behind a table;
- how are you going to speak? Be loud enough to be heard clearly and vary the pace of your delivery. Use variety of tone and pitch as this will prevent you from boring your audience;
- control your nerves; take time and breathe deeply. Be yourself and try to relax and smile; be enthusiastic. Good preparation and practice will aid confidence.

Your material

- gather together the relevant information and put it into logical order, highlighting key points;
- check that your presentation fits into your allotted time for delivery;
- avoid jargon;

- select visual aids, if required, and check that they are clear, precise, relevant, so that they enhance the presentation. Good visual
aids can reinforce your message; add interest and aid understanding. BUT, do not let them dominate. Use visual aids appropriate to
the size of the group. Slides are useful for a larger audience. Do
not talk to your visual aids instead of the audience and do not
have too many. Check that you can handle the apparatus.

Your presentation

- introduce yourself and describe the subject of your presentation
and how long it will take; mention when there will be specific time
allotted for questions. After the presentation, summarise it once
more;
- use notes covering the key points to keep you on track. Cards are
easier to handle than large sheets of paper;
- remember to prepare and practise;
- if you are responding to questions, make sure everyone hears the
question and answer them once, briefly and to the point. If you do
not know the answer, do not make it up, ask for an opportunity to
find out the information.

Your audience

Research the audience to find out:

- who they are
- how many there will be
- what they already know about your subject
- their reason for attending.

Be aware of your audience and their reaction to what you are saying.
You may need to modify your presentation as you proceed, e.g. go over
a point again if further clarification is needed.

The venue

- make sure you are informed about the location so that you are not
late
- check the layout – boardroom, theatre, etc
- ensure that the necessary equipment is available; is a technician
available if needed?
- check the timings and the possibility of prior access to the venue.

Part Three

OTHER INFORMATION

16

PRESS AND PUBLIC RELATIONS

A charity's relationship with the public is very important to the success of its fund-raising activities. People are more likely to give to a charity they have heard something about it; they are even more likely to give if that something is good. Everybody involved with a charity has a PR role to play and should, therefore, be equipped with relevant information about the organisation and its aims. They should present a consistent and positive image of the charity. They should also know when they are *not* the best person to deal with a particular situation or query and to whom they should refer.

Every piece of printed material produced to be seen by any member of the public is communicating the charity's message and purpose (or should be). Therefore this whole issue of public relations needs careful planning and consideration, although when we hear the term public relations or PR we tend to think first of the media – newspapers and other publications, radio and television. The media can work both positively and negatively for a charity; so it is essential to understand the media world.

In this section I am going to look at three areas – people, materials, media – and suggest some ways in which you can make the most of them to ensure that your charity maximises every opportunity to create good PR for itself.

People

The people who work for a charity, whether paid staff or volunteers, on a regular or a one-off basis, will almost certainly have contact with members of the public. They are therefore a PR function of the charity because that contact will help to form the public's opinions and feelings about the cause represented by that particular individual. This is why it is important to ensure that anyone who is representing your charity knows enough about it to be able to deal with situations they are likely to face. This does not mean a volunteer for a street collection knowing all the details of the charity's aims and objectives, but they could well be asked what the charity does, so they should be able to supply the answer to this basis question. It is the responsibility of the organiser of any event or other function of the charity to make sure that everyone concerned has the appropriate level of information and, most importantly, knows where to refer someone who has a specific or detailed enquiry.

The attitude and general demeanour of people representing the charity can affect the way the charity is viewed, so consideration should be given to this when recruiting staff and volunteers. You want people who are going to promote the right image for your charity. You want members of the public to come away from a contact with a representative of your charity feeling positive about the encounter, whatever the level of the particular contact. It is therefore well worth investing some thought and time in your personnel. This investment can range from training to simple briefings, but it should be tailored to the individual. When you hear someone described as a professional fund raiser you will probably automatically think of someone who works for a large charity. But, in my view, the word professional is about the person and not the occupation or employer; it is about the way you do something, about integrity and enthusiasm. Remember that everybody associated with your charity is a valuable member of the team and, as a team member, their attitude and approach to donors really counts.

It is helpful to have one contact point for the media. This could be a dedicated press officer for a larger charity, or merely one person in the organisation who has this as part of their brief. Whatever the case, it is important that the person concerned is well trained in dealing with the media. A consistent approach will be an asset not only for the media contacting the charity, but also for the people within the organisation, who will know exactly to whom to turn with any media enquiries.

Materials

Charities often produce a considerable amount of printed material to fulfil a variety of objectives, ranging from the annual report to a house to house envelope. Every item of literature that is aimed at any section of the public has a PR aspect and should be reviewed with this in mind. Ask yourself if it is putting across the right messages about the charity. Even some items produced for internal purposes, such as volunteer newsletters, are fulfilling a PR function; internal PR has a very important part to play in equipping the charity representatives for their PR role and in making them feel part of the organisation.

A charity should have a corporate identity (logo and its defined use) and corporate colours. If these become recognised by the public they can be a powerful communication tool; so look at materials in this light too. On a national level, I am sure that we would recognise a black and white panda as being the logo for the World Wide Fund for Nature or a red cross as the British Red Cross. The impact of brand recognition for these two charities is manifold; both for casual donors, looking to support a cause in their generic area, and for people remembering these charities in their Will via a legacy – the ultimate gift. There is no reason why you cannot adapt this type of recognition on a local or regional basis ensuring that, through a constant and co-ordinated approach, people begin to recognise and remember your name and identity as being a charity to support locally or regionally in your particular generic area. Indeed, some local causes can gain greater recognition and support locally through a well designed strategy than a national charity ever could. Remember brand recognition is the responsibility of everybody connected with the organisation. It is not something that can be neatly handled by one or two people, although they can certainly lay down the guidelines and ensure that everybody knows what is needed.

A review to ensure that the most has been made of PR opportunities is an effective way of proceeding. For example, in addition to supplying information about the sponsored activity and the space to collect sponsor's names, a sponsor form can also provide information about the charity or cause, e.g. '£X can provide...', 'did you know Y per cent of the population will....', 'in 1995 our charity helped Z thousand people in the UK to ...'. After all, that is what the sponsored event is all about and why, in the main, people have been motivated to help you in the first place.

A brief information leaflet that contains succinct and accessible facts can be a worthwhile investment. It can be used to fulfil many purposes, such as to hand out at events, to include with letters acknowledging donations, etc. The leaflet will furnish information on how to contact the charity – another valuable factor.

With all of the above, include all relevant registered charity information.

Media relations

In the main, the media can be spilt into: television, radio, newspapers and magazines. The first three categories should be divided into local, regional and national sections. Magazines can be divided into specialist, trade, consumer and general publications. But remember, each magazine in the generalist category will have a fairly specific reader and demographic profile of its targeted audience. There are several ways to approach the media in order to highlight a particular newsworthy issue that the charity is promoting. Before you contact the media, however, a certain amount of research is needed. Find out who is the most appropriate person to contact at the local or national newspaper, radio and television station, and keep them informed about the charity's activities. Are there any trade or specialist publications that are appropriate to your charity and its activities? For example, if you are planning a series of events in a particular sport there may be a specific magazine that concentrates on this sport that can provide you with useful information for your event, including possible venues, an annual calendar of events or the name of an appropriate journalist. Make sure you know when the deadline is for inclusion in a particular publication. Are there special supplements on certain days that could be relevant? Does the local radio or television station have a special programme for local events or charity topics? Keep yourself up to date with local and national issues.

This research will allow you to react to circumstances that arise, e.g. if a newspaper runs an article on a subject relevant to your charity, contact them with a comment or response to it. You could do this by simply writing a letter about the article and your charity's views on it which would then be published, or your contact with the newspaper could instigate a follow up article. Ideally you are aiming to establish your charity as an expert on certain relevant topics so that your charity's view will be sought when a journalist is preparing a story. When you are approached for a comment or interview it is important to establish the facts. Do not be afraid to ask questions. You need to know exactly what it is you are commenting on and how your response will be used. If you are asked to do an interview, establish what it is that the journalist is looking for and what angle will be focused upon. If it is a radio or television interview will it be live or recorded? If it is recorded, do not be afraid to ask to re-record something if you are not happy with it. You can also ask to have a tape of the interview. Good preparation for an interview is essential; decide on the most important points you want to put over and make notes; use the full name of the charity – you want the audience to know which organisation you represent. As I have already mentioned, it is helpful for both sides to have a designated and trained individual as the media contact point.

So far, we have looked at PR for the charity in general, but it is likely that you will be wanting to generate PR for specific activities; arguably the most competitive area of media relations. To achieve good coverage for your activity you will have to be pro-active. You will need to look at it from the media's viewpoint – from your research you should know what angles are likely to attract the interest of a particular section of the media and you should present your 'story' with the appropriate slant.

Press releases

These are written communications to specific areas of the media. Releases for local media and magazines should be sent to named individuals; if you do not already have a contact at a particular newspaper or radio station, telephone first to find out to whom your release should be addressed. Having a name means that you can target your release more effectively. You will be able to follow it up with a telephone call to the same person to check the release has been received, to see whether further information is needed and generally to keep your story to the forefront. For the national media, releases should be sent to the News Editor or Forward Planning, since the journalists may work on a shift basis and it may be difficult to contact a particular individual.

A press release should be to the point (ideally one side of A4) and contain all the important information with no jargon or waffle. It is a good idea to include quotes from relevant people in your press release as it gives a human face to a story and looks as if the journalist has actually spoken to the quote provider. It should also be newsworthy. A release should cover – *what* the event or activity is, *who* can get involved or what celebrities are going to be there, *where* it is happening, *when* it is happening, *why* it is happening (to raise money for your charity), *how* people can help and get involved.

All the key information should be contained in the opening paragraph of your release as the news editor may only have time to glance at the first paragraph. Usually a journalist will write the story from the information you have provided. Occasionally, in the regional press, they will use your release as it is, so do consider this when putting it together. The release should be headed Press Release and be presented on paper that identifies the charity. You should date it and give it a title or headline and, if you have to go on to a second page, put *more follows* at the foot of the first page. At the end of your release write *ends*. Anything that appears above this word could be printed; anything after it will not be. Always put the media contact at the charity after the *ends* with telephone, fax and home number. You can also include other notes for the editor at the foot of your release, e.g. you have a corporate sponsor for an event and you would particularly like them mentioned in the piece. Journalists receive numerous releases every day, so do try to make yours different. Consider what is unique or unusual about your event or activity. Is there a human angle you can focus on or a local slant that will make your story that bit more interesting?

It is important that your release arrives in plenty of time. If you are concerned about information being released too soon, your release can be embargoed for a certain day, but this should only be done if essential.

Photographs

A special release can be used to inform the media about a specific photo opportunity that your charity is setting up. It should include the essential *what, where, when, why, who* information, and describe the opportunity. It is basically an invitation to the newspaper to send along a photographer and, ideally, the photocall opportunity should be held between 10.00am and 11.00am, since this suits the picture desks and beats the deadlines on the paper. The release should be sent a week before the event. A successful photocall not only needs to be local and relevant but also needs to have interest and the ability to create a good photograph. Even in local newspapers competition can be fierce for this type of coverage so do try to be different.

Organisation is the key to a good photocall, so on the day make sure that all journalists and photographers are greeted and that their names and details are noted. Then issue them with an information pack, including the press release for the photocall, and relevant information on your charity. Appropriate refreshments will also be well received and will ensure the journalist or photographer leaves your photocall with the right impression.

It is worth considering providing your own photographs for the media. If a celebrity is launching a new appeal, you could have some of your own photographs taken to support your releases. It is a good idea to take photographs at an event; they can be used for the media and they can also be used for future displays or placed in a portfolio to show potential future sponsors. Photographs should be black and white and a good size (8 × 6 inch) for newspapers and colour transparencies for magazines.

Press conferences

If you have important issues to impart to the media, it may be appropriate to invite them to come and hear from you directly and to question you on your news. This approach should be used carefully as it is normally associated with serious news of some consequence. In advance of the press conference you must decide what the issues are and who is going to present them, as well as the general format of the conference. If several people are speaking it may be helpful to appoint a chair to co-ordinate the affair. Timing and venue are particularly important and should be considered well in advance. A thorough press pack should be available for all attendees and should be sent immediately after the press conference to media representatives unable to attend.

Letters campaigns

This is a useful technique for any charity to remember when working with local newspapers, simply write a letter that provides either information on an event or your charity's views on a particular issue. Personalise a copy of this letter to editors of local newspapers. This is also a useful technique for thanking supporters after an event.

Portfolio or guard book

Keep copies of all media articles and mentions, and list down radio and television mentions and appearances in a special portfolio. It will be a useful research document for the charity in the future and it will help you to analyse the success of particular approaches, or the attractiveness to the media of different activities. It will also be invaluable when setting up future appeals or events. You can use your portfolio to show to people you are asking to become involved with your charity. It can prove to a potential sponsor that you are able to deliver media coverage for them if they work with you. It can show a potential venue provider that you have experience in managing similar events successfully.

Crisis PR

It is worth mentioning this area briefly since it is possible for charities to attract negative as well as positive publicity. The media has a responsibility to act as a public watch dog. Any organisation that exists to support a cause with voluntary income is open to this scrutiny and if the media feels there are negative aspects that need to be drawn to the public's attention they will do this. Having an established system of dealing with the crisis situation is essential. Designate a media relations contact who is experienced at dealing with the media and who has developed good relations with them. Reacting honestly, swiftly and consistently allows the charity to respond effectively to negative PR. This is a very complex area of media relations and, when the need arises, it requires expert assistance from specialist consultants.

Celebrities and patrons

Whenever the word *celebrity* is mentioned charities and their committees start to get excited and talk about Joan Collins or Sean Connery opening the local village fête or generally endorsing their fund-raising activities. Celebrities are often associated with charities, but it is essential from the outset to develop realistic expectations of who will be attracted to support your cause. Remember, a celebrity might be the local mayor, the local football or other sports team, a local author or a media star. Ask at the right level for the right cause and you will have more chance of success. Celebrities may request a fee for their attendance at an event, and it is up to the charity to decide on a policy for paying them or not. Whatever the decision, it is usual to pay out of pocket expenses, but do ensure that these are agreed at the outset.

Routes to contacting local celebrities are fairly straightforward, but national and international celebrities may be much more difficult to contact. The appropriate television or film company will be able to provide contact details for the individual's agent. It is always worth looking at who is touring regional theatres and then approaching the theatre, who will be interested in appropriate opportunities as a way of publicising the celebrity's appearance at their theatre.

If you are a medium or large sized charity you may be fortunate enough to have a patron who is either a well known celebrity, business person, member of the peerage or royalty. It is important to consider event opportunities to promote your patron's association with your cause, which increase press interest and possible coverage.

17

USE OF CONSULTANTS AND AGENCIES

Numerous consultancies and agencies exist, covering almost every area of charity and fund raising, from direct mail to databases and strategies to special events. It is likely that at some time most charities, whatever their size or cause, will have considered using an agency or consultant to fulfil an identified need. Many will use them on a regular basis or even have them retained for their charity, others will bring these specialists in from time to time as a particular need arises.

It is therefore reasonable to assume that most organisations involved in fund raising will investigate the consultant and agency market at some time. Before getting involved in the search for the right partner, you will need to establish exactly what you want to achieve by taking on a consultant, and agree why you believe the consultant or agency route is the one to pursue.

So what benefits can a consultant or agency offer?

- they can bring experience of and expertise in a particular area;
- they can offer an objective view;
- they can provide flexibility both in the time given to a project and in the type of input given;
- they can work alongside staff or volunteers who can gain experience and confidence from the association;
- they can be taken on for as long or short a time as needed with no further commitment required;
- they can undertake highly specialised jobs cheaper than the charity.

The cost of employing a consultant or an agency can seem high, with many charging several hundred pounds per day. The majority will charge a daily or project rate, although some may offer to work on a commission basis. Whilst this last option may sound attractive it is not one I would recommend as the costs are less controllable, it is difficult to explain to donors and it is generally not accepted as good practice within the sector. The expenditure involved in employing a consultant has to be considered in the light of what it would cost to cover the work in an alternative way, and how successful and efficient the alternatives are likely to be. It is always possible to use in-house resources, but before doing this you need to be sure that you can free the time required to complete the project and that the necessary expertise is available. You could consider taking on a new member of staff to do the job, but again this longer term commitment and cost needs to be weighed up against the shorter term, more flexible commitment to a consultant.

Once you have decided to take on a consultant or agency, the next thing to consider is which one. This is a very important decision and you should allow yourself time to make the right choice.

There are listings available from many sources like the Institute of Charity Fundraising Managers, the National Council for Voluntary Organisations or Association of Fundraising Consultants and these will provide a good starting point.

You may also be able to acquire useful information from colleagues and other charities about agencies or consultants they have used or of whom they know.

Make yourself a shortlist of about five, and contact them for some initial information. They should provide details of the services they offer, their range of charges and a list of clients, including some that you can contact as referees. This is an important stage of your research and you should take time to follow up these references.

After this information gathering stage, recontact your preferred options, at least two, and invite them in for a preliminary meeting (this should be free of charge), after which they should provide you with an outline of their proposals from the information you have given. Following this they will expect to make a more detailed presentation to you, at which time you should be in a position to make a decision.

A legal contract should be drawn up setting out clearly the terms of the agreement. A sample contract for use with consultants is available from the ICFM and NCVO. This covers all the key areas for consideration when employing a consultant.

A regular review period and evaluation criteria should be established from the outset, to ensure the work is progressing to the expectations and satisfaction of all concerned.

Where consultants or agencies solicit money or property on your behalf, they must comply with Part II of the Charities Act 1992.

18

TAX AND VAT

by Keith Mitchell, Finance Department,
Imperial Cancer Research Fund

Charities are subject to tax and VAT, although there are valuable reliefs available, both to reduce the payments due by a charity and also to recover tax already paid by a donor. Both direct and indirect tax (VAT) are subject to their own regulations and legal framework. This chapter can only give general guidance on tax status and complications that can arise.

The most common ways of tax-efficient giving are considered below.

Deeds of covenant

A legal agreement between the donor and the charity, to pay a specified sum over at least three years.

Collection can be by cash, cheque, standing order or direct debit as frequently as is sensible, e.g. weekly, monthly, quarterly, annually, but full records are required to show the receipt of each instalment. Once the annual sum has been received by the charity, it claims income tax at 25 per cent of the gross sum from the Inland Revenue. For the first year only, the charity requires the donor to complete a simple tax certificate. The donor receives tax relief at their highest rate of income tax, but the charity recovers basic rate tax only. The donor must have taxed income equal to the value of the covenant, otherwise he or she will be faced with a charge by the Revenue equal to the relief given to the charity. As well as being a fairly easy procedure and increasing the value of a covenant by one third, entering into the deed of covenant gives some degree of continuity of support over the term of the deed.

Deposited deed of covenant

This is similar to the instalment deed of covenant described above, except that the donation is paid over as a single sum in a year one as an interest free loan to the charity, and a portion of it is treated as satisfying the deed obligations each year. The donor has to complete a deed of covenant and loan form, but thereafter the administration is handled by the charity. The use of deposited covenants has declined with the introduction of Gift Aid (see below) but has value for those donors who wish to donate in excess of their annual taxable income, and gives the cash flow advantage of receipt in full.

Gift Aid

A donor giving over £250 as a single donation can complete a simple certificate which gives tax treatment equivalent to a covenant but within one year. The donor receives relief on such donations and the charity can recover basic rate tax paid by the donor. The charity recovers tax equivalent to one third of the donation. The donor must have taxed income at least equal to the amount of the donation within the tax year of the donation, otherwise a charge will be levied by the Revenue to recover the relief given to the charity. This is a simple means of increasing the value to the charity of a single donation of £250.00 to £333.33.

Each of the forms of giving described above relates to donations made by donors from their post tax income to a charity, which can then recover a sum equivalent to the basic rate income tax on the value of the donation, and the donor can deal directly with the charity. Giving can also be achieved, however, through organisations acting as agents that encourage giving to charity in general. For example, Charities Aid Foundation receives donations by covenant, deposited covenant or Gift Aid, and recovers the tax as appropriate. After their handling charges, they hold a pool of gross money available for distribution by the donor to any registered charity by CAF voucher, CAF Charity Card or direct instructions to CAF to distribute the funds. Any such donation cannot be used for payment of covenant or Gift Aid – as the tax has already been recovered – nor for payment of goods or services.

CAF is the largest organisation providing this service.

Payroll giving

For employees paying income tax under the PAYE scheme, whose employers have established a payroll giving scheme, only. The donor instructs his or her employer to deduct (max £900 pa) the donation from wages or salary, prior to tax being calculated. The employer then passes the deduction to a payroll giving agency, which distributes the donations to the charity or charities specified by the employee. The donation received by the charity is gross of tax, and cannot be used to pay instalments under a deed of covenant or Gift Aid, or as payment for goods or services.

There are costs of such a scheme to the employer, but payroll giving can be used in links with corporate donations, and also creates an ongoing relationship between the charity and donor, if the donor consents to details of name and address being passed to the charity.

Legacy giving

Any gift to a charity under a Will is free of inheritance tax, whether cash or goods, specific or a share of the residue of the estate. The charity cannot recover any tax on such gifts, but is entitled to recover its share of any income tax paid by the executors during the period of their administration. Use of gifts to charity can reduce the value of the estate to below the inheritance tax threshold. Gifts can only arise from valid Wills, however – laws of intestacy do not allow charitable donations – hence the encouragement by charities to make a Will.

Gifts in kind

Tax-efficient giving examples above relate solely to gifts of money, except for legacy giving, which can be money or goods. However, the gift to a charity of an asset that is subject to capital gains tax prevents the crystalisation of the gain, and when sold by the charity is exempt tax. For example, a donor owns a picture valued at £10,000 which cost £1,000. If the donor sells the picture, capital gains tax of 25 per cent $\times$ £9,000 is payable and the charity receives £7,750. If the donor gives the picture to the charity, which then sells it for £10,000, the charity receives the full £10,000.

Tax-efficient giving for companies

This chapter has so far considered gift by individuals only; the tax-efficient giving methods available to companies are: (i) covenants, (ii) deposited covenants and (iii) Gift Aid. The procedures are identical, except that companies have no minimum value of Gift Aid donation and every donation must pass through the Gift Aid regulations. Companies are responsible for paying income tax at 25 per cent of the gross donation under the CT61 reporting requirements, but such income tax paid is available for offset against their corporation tax liability once agreed.

Although Gift Aid is easy, there are advantages to covenants for certain companies – particularly trading subsidiaries of charities or those companies wishing to donate a percentage of their profits.

Payroll giving and legacy giving are not applicable to companies.

Companies can also make gifts in kind tax efficiently by giving items with a potentially taxable gain which would be taxed if the item were sold (as described in the example quoted above). Companies can also obtain relief against their corporation tax liability for gifts to charity of items of trading stock, or some specific items given to certain types of charities. For example, the gift of computer equipment previously used by a company to a school. Useful reference in this area is given in the *Craigmyle Guide to Charitable Giving and Taxation*.

Value Added Tax (VAT)

VAT is a tax on goods and services which is collected by registered persons and paid to the Government of the United Kingdom on a quarterly basis. Registration is required for organisations with business income exceeding the annual threshold – set by the annual Finance Act. The registration will include all associated bodies together with the main charity, e.g branches, groups, etc.

Business income is the key information to determine VAT status, and this can be generally regarded as being equivalent to sales, whether of goods or a service. For example, the sale of a ticket for a dinner dance is business income, as the dinner could be purchased from a non-charitable organisation. The sum of all such business income must be monitored, and if anticipated income exceeds the registration threshold, the organisation needs to register for VAT. If not registered then, regardless of activity, no VAT is chargeable but also no VAT paid on expenses, etc, can be recovered.

The identification of business income is critical to status and all cases need to be identified. For example, is the gift from a corporate body actually a philanthropic gift or do they receive free advertising in return for their money or goods? Each type of fund raising should be reviewed for the benefit passing to the giver, other than mere acknowledgement of the gift.

If the fund raising proposed takes business income over the registration level, or the fund raising is an integral part of a charity registered for VAT, then the VAT status of the event needs to be recognised and reported as legislation requires. Not all business income is charged at positive VAT rates, being split between standard rated, zero rated or exempt. These are reviewed below:

Standard rated income

Supplying organisation charges 17.5 per cent of selling prices and pays this over to the central government. VAT on costs incurred is recoverable from the government.

Zero rated income, e.g. sale of books, children's clothes, donated goods

No charge to the customer, any VAT incurred is recoverable.

Exempt income

No charge to the customer, but VAT incurred is not recoverable. This aspect increases the costs of generating the income.

In an attempt to reduce VAT administration, certain events which would otherwise be regarded as taxable are treated as exempt when arranged by a charity or trading subsidiary owned by a charity, as one off fund-raising events. One off meaning up to three times per annum for the same event in the same location for major events, except for those when the income is not raised primarily as a charitable donation, e.g. celebrity attending premieres. VAT status of all income generating events should be checked as if the recovery of VAT on costs incurred is not possible, the net result of the event can be substantially affected.

Trading

Having identified the VAT status of the funds being raised, the profits of the event may be subject to tax. Part of the standard constitutional requirement of a charity is a prohibition on permanent trading. The Revenue however also gives exemption from tax for certain specific trades, these being: trade in pursuance of a primary purpose of the charity or involving the beneficiaries of the charity: or (by concession) small scale events such as jumble sales, coffee mornings, etc. The regulations for exemption from direct tax do not match the VAT exemption of one off fund-raising events, although recent editions of the explanatory notes from Customs and Excise and the Inland Revenue have introduced more similarity.

The exemption to tax (regardless of the VAT status) will not cover all trading ventures proposed, and some of these will either face a tax charge or be organised via a third party to avoid such a charge. The most frequently used vehicle is a trading subsidiary. This separate legal entity is normally wholly owned by the charity and undertakes various trading activities, such as the sale of Christmas cards etc. While subject to the same VAT regulations as the charity, the profits of such a company are taxable under corporation tax, unless tax saving measures are introduced – these can be dividends, covenant or Gift Aid. On reflection, the most efficient is a variable deed of covenant, but this needs an estimated sum paid up to the charity prior to the end of the company's tax period (such sum can be reduced to actual after the tax computation for the company has been agreed with the Inland Revenue).

The cost benefit examination of establishing a separate company, with legal, audit and additional administration costs, needs to be made for each charity. If a subsidiary is established, the fund raising should clarify whether the event is run by the charity or the company. The company cannot receive donations or CAF vouchers, deeds of covenant or Gift Aid payments – nor give consideration for such gifts to the charity.

This chapter can only summarise in general terms the tax and VAT position of charitable fund raising in the UK. Matters of doubt should be clarified with Customs & Excise (re VAT) and the Inland Revenue (re tax) or by taking professional advice.

APPENDIX I

ICFM Codes of Practice and Guidance Notes

What is available includes:

- fund raising in schools;
- standard form of agreement between charities and fund-raising consultants;
- reciprocal charity mailings;
- house-to-house collections;
- telephone recruitment of collectors;
- the management of static collection boxes;
- outbound telephone support.

For any of the above, contact the ICFM directly. Please note, a small charge may apply.

APPENDIX II

—— NRS Social grade definitions* ——

Social grade	Social status	Occupation
A	Upper middle class	Higher managerial administrative or professional
B	Middle class	Intermediate managerial administrative or professional
C1	Lower middle class	Supervisory or clerical, and junior managerial, administrative or professional
C2	Skilled working class	Skilled manual workers
D	Working class	Semi- and unskilled manual workers
E	Those at lowest level of subsistence	State pensioners or widows (no other earner), casual or lowest-grade workers

* These are the standard social grade classifications using definitions agreed between Research Services Ltd and National Readership Surveys Ltd. They are described in an NRS publication *Social Grading on the National Readership Survey*.

These are the standard social grade classifications used in the United Kingdom; they will vary from other classifications used in Europe and the rest of the world, but all countries have such a classification system. When planning events, and particularly when talking to companies, it is useful to be familiar with the above as these terms are commonly used.

Source: NRS, National Readership Surveys Ltd

APPENDIX III

—————— Useful addresses ——————

Action Resource Centre	1st Floor 102 Park Village East London NW1 3SP	0171 383 2200
Advertising Standards Authority	Brook House 2/16 Torrington Place London WC1E 7HW	0171 580 5555
Angal Products	68 First Avenue Twickenham SW14 8SR	0181 788 5464
Arts Council	National Lottery Dept 14 Great Peter Street London SW1P 3NQ	0171 312 0123 Non lottery: 0171 333 0100
Association for Business Sponsorship of the Arts (ABSA)	Nutmeg House 60 Gainsford Street London SE1 2NY	0171 378 8143
Association of Fund Raising Consultants	The Grove Harpenden Herts AL5 1AH	01582 762441

BBC Appeals Office	Broadcasting House Portland Place London W1A 1AA	0171 580 4468
BBC Children in Need Appeal	Broadcasting Support Services First Floor Villiers House Ealing London W5 2PA	0181 280 8000
British Institute of Management	Management House Cottingham Road Corby Northants NN17 1TT	01536 201651
Burnett Associates	74/77 White Lion Street London N1 9PF	0171 833 2154
Business in the Community	8 Stratton Street London W1X 5FD	0171 629 1600
Charities Advisory Trust	Radius Works Back Lane London NW3 1HL	0171 794 9835
Charities Aid Foundation (CAF)	48 Pembury Road Tonbridge Kent TN9 2JD	01732 771333
Charity Commission	St Alban's House 57-60 Haymarket London SW1Y 4QX	0171 210 3000

Charity Forum	60 Laurel Avenue Potters Bar Herts EN6 2AB	01707 662448
Charity Projects	74 New Oxford Street London WC1A 1EF	0171 436 1122
Charity Recruitment (Incorporating CR Consultants)	40 Rosebery Avenue London EC1R 4RN	0171 833 0770 0171 833 0414
Charity Shop Services	15 High Street Alconbury Huntingdon Cambs PE17 5DS	01480 890261
Community Matters	8/9 Upper Street London N1 0PQ	0171 226 0189
Community Service Volunteers	237 Pentonville Road London N1 9NJ	0171 278 6601
Companies House (personal callers)	55/71 City Road London EC1Y 1BB	0171 253 9393
(queries)	Crown Way Maindy Cardiff CF4 3UZ	01222 380801
Confederation of British Industries (CBI)	103 New Oxford Street London WC1A 1DU	0171 379 7400
Craigmyle & Co Ltd	The Grove Harpenden Herts AL5 1AH	01582 762441

Data Protection Registrar	Springfield House Water Lane Wilmslow Cheshire SK9 5AF	01625 535777
Directory of Social Change (DOSC)	24 Stephenson Way London NW1 2DP	0171 209 5151
EC Commission	Rue de la Loi 200 1049 Brussels Belgium	00 32 2 35 11 11
EC Commission London Office	8 Storey's Gate London SW1P 3AT	0171 973 1992
Gaming Board for Great Britain	Berkshire House 168/173 High Holborn London WC1V 7AA	0171 306 6200
Independent Television Commission (ITC)	70 Brompton Road London SW3 1EY	0171 584 7011
Inland Revenue	Charity Division (England, Wales & N Ireland) St John's House Merton Road Bootle Merseyside L69 9BB	0151 472 6000
Inland Revenue	Charity Division (Scotland) Trinity House South Trinity Road Edinburgh EH5 3SD	0131 552 6255

Institute of Charity Fundraising Managers (ICFM)	Market Towers 1 Nine Elms Lane London SW8 5NQ	0171 627 3436
Institute of Public Relations	The Old Trading House 15 Northburgh Street London EC1V 0PR	0171 253 5151
Institute of Sales Promotions	Arena House 66/68 Pentonville Road London N1 9HS	0171 837 5340
Local Government Information Unit	1/5 Bath Street London EC1V 9QQ	0171 608 1051
Management Centre	65 Westgate Road Newcastle upon Tyne NE1 1SG	0191 222 1632
	366 Kennington Road London SE11 4DB	0171 820 1100
Millenium Commission	2 Little Smith Street London SW1P 3DH	0171 340 2001
National Association for Volunteer Bureaux	St Peter's College College Road Saltley Birmingham B8 3TE	0121 327 0265
National Council for Voluntary Organisations (NCVO)	Regent's Wharf 8 All Saints Street London N1 9RL	0171 713 6161
National Heritage Memorial Fund	Head of Lottery 10 St James' Street London SW1A 1EF	0171 930 0963

National Lottery Charities Board	7th Floor St Vincent House 30 Orange Street London WC2H 7HH	0171 839 5371
Northern Ireland Office	Stormont Castle Stormont Estate Belfast BT4 3ST	01232 235111
Payroll Giving Association	231 Kennington Lane London SE11 5QU	0171 820 1699
Peekes of Bournemouth	Riverside Lane Tuckton Bournemouth Dorset BH6 3LD	01202 417777
Press Association Ltd	85 Fleet Street London EC4P 4BE	0171 353 7440
Professional Fundraising Magazine	4 Market Place Hertford SG14 1EB	01992 501177
Retired Executives Action Clearing House (REACH)	Bean Wharf 27 Bankside London SE1 9PD	0171 928 0452
Scottish Office	St Andrew's House Regent Road Edinburgh EH1 3DE	0131 556 8400

Smee & Ford Ltd	2nd Floor St George's House 195/203 Waterloo Road London SE1 8XD	0171 928 4050
Sports Council	National Lottery Unit PO Box 649 London WC1H 0QP	0171 388 1277
Third Sector Magazine	4 Assam Street London E1 7QS	0171 247 0066
Trustee Register	Reed Charity 53 Peascod Street Windsor Berks SL4 1DE	01753 868277
Voluntary Services Unit	Home Office 50 Queen Anne's Gate London SW1H 9AT	0171 273 3571
Volunteer Centre UK	Carriage Row 183 Eversholt Street London NW1 1BU	0171 388 9888
Webb Ivory Ltd	Primrose Hill Preston Lancs PR1 4EZ	01772 204444
Welsh Office	Crown Buildings Cathays Park Cardiff CF1 3NQ	01222 825111

APPENDIX IV

—— Sample deed of covenant ——

(NB Applies to England and Wales only)

Please return this form to:- Covenants Department, [*address of your charity*]

STARTING A COVENANT

If you pay income tax, a covenant increases the value of your contribution to the [*Name of your charity*] by one third without costing you a penny. As a registered charity, we can reclaim the income tax you have already paid on the value of your covenant. Simply fill in the form below and return it to us – not your bank – in the envelope provided.

Should you require assistance or advice in the completion of this form, simply call our covenant helpline on [*include a phone number*].

I (Mr/ Mrs/ Miss/ Ms/ Title) . . . .
(*Full name, in capitals please*)
of (*Full postal address*) . . . .
. . . . Postcode. . . . .
promise to pay the [*Name of your charity*] for . . . . .years (this must be a minimum of four years), or during my life (if shorter) the sum that will, after deduction of income tax at basic rate, amount to:
£ . . . . (*figures*). . . . .(*words*)
(*Insert the amount you wish to give*)
Monthly/ Quarterly/ Annually (*Delete as appropriate*)
Starting on . . . ./. . . . . . ./. . . . . . (*This date must be on or after the date you sign the deed*)
Signed and delivered . . . . (Signature) . . . . (Date)
Witness's name . . . . (*In capitals please*)

Witness's address...
....Postcode ....
Witness's signature ....

BANKERS ORDER

To the Manager..........................(*name of your bank*)
at (*bank address*) ....
.... Postcode
Bank sort code: ☐☐ ☐☐ ☐☐
Account number ☐☐☐☐☐☐☐☐
Please pay the (*Your charity name*)
£ ....(*figures*)................................(*words*)
Monthly/ Quarterly/ Annually (*Delete as appropriate*)
Starting on ..... /..../.......... up to and including/..........
or
Starting on ..../........./ .... until further notice
(*Delete as appropriate*)
Payable to [*Your bank address and sort code*] for the credit of the [*Your charity name and account number*]
Name ....
                    Signature .... Date ....
                    [*Your Registered Charity Number*]

—— Event feasibility review ——

EVENT:

DATE:

VENUE (or options):

Responsibility:

Event objective:

Budget: £ . . . .

Estimated gross income	£	Estimated gross expenditure	£
Ticket sales		Venue hire	
Donations		Entertainment (1)	
Raffle		Entertainment (2)	
Sponsorship		Catering	
Incidental		Printing	
Other		Postage	
		Marketing (1)	
		Marketing (2)	
		Consultants	
		Flowers	
		Prizes	
		Other	
Total:		**Total:**	

Estimated net income: [*gross income minus expenditure*]

Estimated hours:

Professional staff - - - - - - - -   @ £ . . . . . . per hour = £

  Support staff - - - - - - - -   @ £ . . . . . . per hour = £

    Volunteers - - - - - - - -   @ £ . . . . . . per hour = £

  Total Hours: **Total approximate cost:** £

Estimated net income after staff costs: | £ |

Type of event (e.g. Sale, Sponsor, Integrated, Ticket):

Essential elements/ features:

Will the event run without a sponsor?

What is the breakeven point? (e.g. number of tickets):

What could go wrong? (e.g. weather, artist, etc.):

What are the competitive events in the market place?

Will this appeal to existing groups of supporters?

Who are we targeting and how?

What media coverage is needed?

What are the lead-in times?

Other comments:

Gifts in kind expected:

Item	**Donor**	**Value**

Signed: .... Date: ....

APPENDIX V

Reference books

BRAD Advertiser and Agency List, BRAD

Debrett's Distinguished People of Today, Debrett's Peerage Ltd

Debrett's Peerage, Debrett's Peerage Ltd

Dimensions of the Voluntary Sector, Charities Aid Foundation

Directory of Directors, Thomas Skinner Directories

Directory of Grant Making Trusts, Charities Aid Foundation

Guide to Company Giving, Directory of Social Change

Guide to Major Trusts, Directory of Social Change

Henderson's Top 2000 Charities, Hemmington Scott

Hollis Press and PR Annual, Hollis

Hollis Sponsorship and Donations Yearbook, Hollis

Key British Enterprises, Dunn & Bradstreet

MacMillan's Unquoted Companies, MacMillan

Major Companies and Their Charitable Giving, Directory of Social Change

Management of Voluntary Organisations, Croner's

Millionaire Givers, Directory of Social Change

Stock Exchange Official Yearbook

Times 1000, Times Books

Tolley's Charities Manual, Tolley Publishing Co

Who's Who, A & C Black

Further reading

Arts Funding Guide, Doulton, Directory of Social Change

Business Policy, G. Luffman and S. Sanderson, Blackwell Business

Charity Appeals, Marion Allford, J M Dent

Complete Fundraising Handbook, Sam Clarke, Directory of Social Change

Craigmyle Guide to Charitable Giving and Taxation, Craigmyle and Co Ltd

Education Grants Directory, L. FitzHerbert and M. Eastwood, Directory of Social Change

Environmental Grants, Susan Forrester, Directory of Social Change

Filthy Rich and Other Non Profit Fantasies, Dr Richard Steckel, Ten Speed Press

High Street Giving, Stephen Humble, Directory of Social Change

How to Write Letters That Sell, C. Godefroy and D. Glocheux, Judy Piatkus Publishing

Managing the Non Profit Organisation, Peter Drucker, Butterworth Heinemann

Marketing Plan, M. McDonald and P. Morris, Heinemann Professional Publishing

Master Marketeer, Christopher Ryan, Kogan Page Ltd

Pinpointing Affluence, Judith Nichols, Precept Press Inc

Planning for the Future, N. Martin and C. Smith, NCVO Publications

Raising Money from Trusts, Michael Norton, Directory of Social Change

Relationship Fundraising, Ken Burnett, White Lion Press Ltd

Sales Promotion, Julian Cummins, Kogan Page Ltd

Strategies for Success, H Barnard and P. Walker, NCVO Publications

Targeted Fund Raising, Judith Nichols, Precept Press Inc

The Emerging Sector, L. Salamon and H. Anheier, Johns Hopkins University

The Fundraising Cycle, Redmond Mullin, Redmond Mullin Ltd

Trading by Charities, Keith Mitchell, Charities Tax Reform Group

Publications

Charity, Charities Aid Foundation

Professional Fundraising, Brainstorm Publishing Ltd

Third Sector, Third Sector Publications

Update, Institute of Charity Fundraising Managers

INDEX